$34.95

MW01168740

$34.95

Images
of the
San Juans

Historic Selections from the Ruth and Marvin Gregory Photograph Collection

by P. David Smith

Western Reflections Inc.
Ouray, Colorado

Published by:

Western Reflections Inc.

P.O. Box 710
Ouray, Colorado 81427
U. S. A.

First printing 1997
Printed in the United States of America

Library of Congress Cataloging-in-Publication Data
Smith, P. David
    *Images of the San Juans - Historical Selections from
    the Ruth and Marvin Gregory Photograph Collection*
    Includes Index

    1. Colorado History   I. Title

Library of Congress Catalog Card No. 97-60563
ISBN 1-890437-12-3

Cover design, book design and typography:
Pat Wilson, *Country Graphics*

First Edition

Dedicated to the memory of Marvin Gregory
We Miss Him Very Much.

CONTENTS

PREFACE

The book that you are holding in your hands is a compilation of photographs but it is not just any collection of photographs. It is an assemblage of historical images from one of the most scenic and historic spots in the United States — the San Juan Mountains of Southwestern Colorado. These scenes were collected by Ruth and Marvin Gregory — a couple who greatly love the beauty and the history of the San Juans. Marvin passed away in 1992. Ruth Gregory supplied much of the information about the photographs. To this, Ouray historian P. David Smith has added his knowledge of local history and has written the captions.

Within these pages are selections from thousands of images that comprise the Gregory's collection. The photos have been collected for over fifty years. Some are purely artistic photographs. Most, however, are both historically interesting and pleasing. P. David Smith also presents the story behind the scene. In most cases the Gregorys own the original negatives (many of which are glass plates) from which these prints have been made. In some instances they made copy negatives from the original photographs — some of which they own and some of which were copied with permission from others. Besides photographic prints, some of the negatives were copies of scenes from books, newspapers, stereographs, drawings, artifacts and many other sources that became available to them. They took many of the photographs themselves. Some were taken by others and, where known, are cited. Some of the images have greater artistic value; some have greater historical value. Quite a number of the negatives produce razor sharp images, some are dull and blurry. A few of the photographs are even a combination of both fuzzy and clear images because of the distortion of the early camera lens. An effort has been made to make the reproduction as clear as possible, but an out-of-focus image cannot be focused and a print that is missing a part of its image cannot be replaced. Every effort was made to use clear and sharp photographs. In some cases the importance of the content of the image has greatly outweighed the quality of the photograph. We know that you will find them all interesting and unique.

Both Ruth and David learned long ago that one's conception of past history is constantly changing. The actual facts never change, of course; but information constantly evolves that discloses new truths. For example, in many cases Ruth and David have had to rely on information written on the backs of old prints, and that information may or may not be correct. They encourage your input if you know a statement to be wrong or have additional information to pass along. Of course, the photos themselves never lie even though the eye might be deceived. We are always looking, always learning, and we welcome new information.

One of the ways that Ruth supplements her income is to make copies of her historical prints. If you enjoy a photograph and would like to have a copy of it, we would encourage you to contact Ruth or David in Ouray, Colorado. If you have additional historical images that you would like to share with us, we would appreciate a chance to see them.

Most of all we hope that you will come to love the San Juans as we have — in all their majestic and awe-inspiring beauty and wrapped in a cloak of historical fact that rivals that of any other area in the United States. It is easy for historical circumstance to become a living, breathing experience in the San Juan country. We hope that you will see and feel the history of the San Juans in this volume and enjoy reading it as much as we enjoyed putting it together.

INTRODUCTION
MEET RUTH AND MARVIN GREGORY

Practically every historian in the state of Colorado knows the names of Ruth and Marvin Gregory. For over forty years their photographic collection has been freely opened to anyone expressing any serious interest in illustrating manuscripts, embellishing articles or perhaps just adding to the family album. Countless numbers of people have learned to love the San Juans and its colorful history through the striking images that the generous Gregorys have shared. To Marvin and Ruth the images on the paper are living and breathing history. They have always had an uncanny way of looking at a photograph and bringing it to life. "Look at that house on the hill, it's the 'sick' house." "See the emblems on the horses — that 'A' is for Ashenfelter." "Notice the ore sacks piled up by the side of the house." You are drawn back into other ages as Marvin or Ruth explain the photographs to you. Unlike memories that can fade and stories that can grow, photographs always tell the truth — one always views the authentic past.

This photo of Marvin and Ruth was taken just shortly before Marvin's death. He wore a button that read: "Beware. Talkative Old Bastard." The button was the result of a comment made in a local book about Marvin's love of talking with others. Marvin did love to talk, especially about history; but the button was obviously just a joke, showing that Marvin had no trouble laughing at himself — a quality that we would all do well to learn.

Marvin died in 1992 and Ruth is now in her eighties. In part, this book tells a quick story of their lives but, just as importantly, it tells the story of many of their favorite photographs. A few of the images were actually taken by the Gregorys. Most, however, come from thousands of photographs that they collected over a fifty-year period along with many photographic and historic artifacts. They believe strongly in privately owned historical photograph collections, yet they are always quick to provide museums with copies of any important photos. The Gregorys try to name the photographer or collector, if known — "This one is Grant Marcy's," "This was taken by Frank Rice" or "My friend Connie Johnson sent me this one."

Ruth became interested in collecting historic photographs through a love of the genealogy of her family —now in its sixth generation in the San Juans. Many photos in the Gregory collection are straight out of her family photo album. Ruth's mother, Luella Shaw, wrote a diary of her experiences in the San Juans during the early 1900s. Luella also researched the family's genealogy — going back in detail through five generations. In 1909, she wrote a book on Colorado history entitled *True History of Some of the Pioneers of Colorado*. It is now a rare and sought-after collection of stories told to her by "old-timers" — many of whom were her own relatives.

Ruth's photographs are especially important to her since either she or her family actually lived the life that many of the photographs chronicle. Her great-grandfather, John W. Shaw, came to Colorado in 1863. He and his family were reportedly the first whites to establish a homestead in the vicinity of what is now Pueblo, Colorado. The Shaws were in constant danger of being attacked by Indians. So great was the risk that John kept a wagon and team by his front door, ready to take his family to the nearby fort at any sign of hostilities. In 1876 the family moved to Parrott City, which is now a ghost town but was originally located between present-day Durango and Cortez, Colorado. Later the Shaws moved to Animas City (now a part of Durango) where John built the settlement's first house and then expanded it into a hotel called the Shaw House. The Shaws also helped to build the first church in southwestern Colorado. Ruth's paternal grandparents, Charles and Ellen Shaw, were married in 1881 and also lived in Animas City. The Shaw family faced many dangers over several decades during the frontier days of Colorado.

Ruth Gregory's family goes back for six generations in the San Juans. John Shaw was Ruth's great-grandfather. Front row, left to right: Mrs. John Shaw (born Almina Holt on May 25, 1833 in Elmina, New York) married John on August 15, 1850; Charles Byron Shaw, born in Des Moines, Iowa on February 2, 1856; Minnie Shaw, born in Pueblo, Colorado on October 6, 1865 and married in 1890 in Animas City, Colorado to Henry Bolinger; Ellen Shaw, born May of 1864 in Pueblo, Colorado and married Lt. B. N. Waters of the U. S. Army in Durango, Colorado on July 30, 1880 (Lt. Waters was probably in the area because of the Ute scare culminating in the Meeker Massacre); and John W. Shaw, born April 19, 1827 in Albany, New York. Back row, left to right: Emma L. Shaw born in Nebraska on March 16, 1859 and married Thomas Hicklin, grandson of Col. Bent, builder of Bent's Fort near Pueblo, Colorado on October 24, 1881; Louisa Shaw, born June 5, 1851 in Illinois and married Dr. Peter R. Tombs in Pueblo on August 29, 1870; and Frank Shaw (a woman and not short for Francie or Francis), born March 19, 1870 and married Charlie Wigglesworth in Animas City.

Ruth's mother, Luella Shaw, was one of five children born to Charles and Ellen. In 1895 Charles moved to Silverton, Colorado where he worked as a packer and freighter. Luella went to school in nearby Howardsville and later graduated from Silverton High School. When her brother, Clarence, developed heart problems that were aggravated by the high altitude, Ellen, Luella and Clarence moved to the farming settlement of Hotchkiss, Colorado (Charles stayed in Silverton); and it was there that Ruth's mother married. Ruth was born on February 11, 1911. Most of the family eventually returned to the Silverton-Eureka-Howardsville area, and Ruth still vividly remembers the high valley's harsh winters and deep snows. Ruth attended the first grade in Eureka (now a ghost town) before returning to Hotchkiss for the rest of her schooling.

Fate brought Marvin into the picture. Marvin was born May 13, 1911, into a Quaker family in Osborne County, Kansas. He moved to Hotchkiss, Colorado in the sixth grade. Ruth and Marvin were then in the same class all the way through high school. They even went to the same church and sang in the choir together. Marvin would usually walk Ruth home after choir practice, and they graduated together in 1930. Although they always liked each other, there was no real love affair until shortly before their marriage on November 11, 1933. It was during the heart of the depression and times were hard — very hard. Marvin proposed after one of their long walks towards the adobe hills near Hotchkiss. Ruth still chuckles as she remembers that he said, "If you don't marry me, you'll just have to walk home alone." Ruth responded, "Well, then... I might just take you up on that."

Marvin worked on a ranch on Rogers Mesa (just outside Hotchkiss) during his summers in high school. Ruth helped her family run a "soup kitchen" — a place where the workers at the nearby fruit packing house could come get a sandwich, a bowl of soup, a candy bar or something to drink during their breaks. At the time of their marriage, Marvin was working as a stock and delivery boy at a local grocery store making one to two dollars a day. About a year later he was sent to Grand Junction, Colorado to apprentice as a butcher. Money was so tight that, except on very special occasions, Ruth and Marvin couldn't come up with a spare dime each to go to the movies. When Marvin was offered a better job in Paonia, Colorado, he and Ruth were quick to move; but since the customers only wanted to barter for their meat (and the Gregorys needed cash), they moved again to nearby Cedaredge. The new job not only meant more money but, just as important to Marvin, his brother couldn't keep bugging him to let him borrow his automobile. As it turned out, he had to sell his automobile anyway to make ends meet.

Marvin and Ruth moved to Ouray, Colorado in the spring of 1936 when he took a job at the Nickel and Smith Butcher Shop (now a part of Duckett's Market). It was then that the

These women were waiting for Marvin's slide show to begin. They were evidently in a group that had come to enjoy the show in the 1950s. The slide show was held in the Gregory's Vistaland operation. The piano had a sign on it that read: "If you play the piano, please do."

Gregorys began to be introduced to the lure of historic photography. As Ruth puts it: "After seeing Box Canyon, Cascade Falls and the goldfish pond down by the swimming pool, Marvin was told that there was a small museum across from City Hall, which we might enjoy. It was run by a kindly, older gentleman named Grant Marcy. We spent many Sunday afternoons at his museum that summer. It was the beginning of a wonderful friendship." Grant Marcy had originally come to Leadville, Colorado in the early 1890s, then moved to the Camp Bird Mine near Ouray in 1900. After ten more years he came down to Ouray to open a small photographic studio.

When Grant Marcy died, the mortician found that he had left typed notes attached to most of his historic photographs and artifacts that read "Property of Marvin Gregory."

Ruth and Marvin's son, Noel, was born in Hotchkiss in 1934 and their sons, Eddie and Elwood, were born in Ouray in 1937 and 1939 respectively. Marvin gradually worked into doing carpentry work at night. He loved working with stone and wood and by 1942 he was doing it full time. Foundations and stonework were his specialty. At age 13, Noel became interested in photography and Ruth greatly encouraged him in that interest. They would walk down to Babe Snyder and Frank Massard's Corner Drug Store (now the Ouray Variety Store) to buy their film and equipment. Soon Ruth was doing her own film developing and printing, at first by taking a quilt and tacking it over the a small window to create a darkroom. She used a kerosene lantern with a red globe for a light. Later the back porch of their home was turned into the dark room.

In the very early fifties, Marvin started driving for Buddy Davis' high mountain tours. It was a new industry, which was made possible by the availability of the four-wheel-drive World War II army surplus jeep. The few tourists that wandered into Ouray were awe-struck by the natural and man-made wonders they would see along the old wagon roads. Sometimes Ruth would accompany Marvin on his tours, and she would of-

This photo was taken high in the mountains in the 1950s. Ruth was at rear right and Elwood Gregory at left. Marvin was taking the photo. During this part of their life the Gregorys spent as much time as possible in the high country of the San Juans taking slides and photographs which they sold in their store or used in their slide shows.

ten take slides of the marvelous mountain scenery. The tourists were frantically taking snapshots in every direction and soon Marvin was taking slides and photographs, too. It didn't take long before Marvin had an idea — make slides of their growing collection of old photographs and mix in slides they had taken of the high country so as to make a show for the tourists. There would be no charge for the show; it would promote the high mountain scenery of the Ouray area, be something for the tourists to do at night and, best of all, allow Marvin and Ruth a chance to talk with new and old friends.

In the summer of 1954, the Gregorys opened a little photography shop in Ouray. Their main purpose was to help their son Noel, then 19, continue with his photography career. Their first slide show production was in a building that had most recently been Amy Massard's steam laundry and before that the infamous Bucket of Blood Saloon. It was located on the corner of Fifth Avenue and Main Street. After 1955 Ruth and Marvin operated a gift store and slide show next door to the south. Besides selling film, Noel continued to do film developing and the family sold enlargements of both their new and historic photographs. The first summer it was presented, the show mainly consisted of slides the Gregorys borrowed from Buddy Davis. At the beginning of that summer there were sometimes only four or five people at each show watching Marvin and Ruth's efforts. By fall, there were as many as thirty or forty guests at each showing.

By the second year the production was composed mainly of the Gregorys' own work and the crowds grew substantially. Their historic photograph collection also began to grow as they made copies of the rare photographs that people would bring to them after viewing the show. The Gregorys eventually moved their operation to the Masonic Lodge building across the street and finally into a room at the Wright's Opera House. Each move provided more and more space for their audiences, but they still ended up with people standing at the door, looking in windows and seated on the stairs. For seventeen years the slide show ran — always free and without any type of commercialism. Marvin, after being told enough times that he was crazy for not charging admission, did eventually put an old trunk by the front door with a slot cut in the top for donations.

Ruth Gregory is an accomplished artist – both with oils and with a camera. Here she was working on an oil painting of the amphitheater at Ouray, which is basically the scene that she has seen out the front window of her house for over fifty years. The painting now hangs at the Ouray County Historical Museum.

After the store closed, Noel went on to become a professional photographer in Colorado Springs. Ruth had, in the meanwhile, come to love the printing and enlarging of photographs herself — "to see the images coming alive right before my eyes!" It was another chance to continue to collect additional photographs from people who needed copies or who just sent them photographs of the San Juans that had been discovered all over the United States. Their collection grew to thousands of images and began to draw the attention of historic writers from all over the country. As an example of the size of their collection, it took over one hundred hours just to chose the photographs for this book. The Gregorys' photographs have appeared in perhaps a hundred books, sometimes under the caption "The Marvin Gregory Collection," sometimes "The Ruth Gregory Collection" and sometimes "The Ruth and Marvin Gregory Collection." Ruth says that it made no difference to them how they were credited.

Besides photography Ruth loves to write poetry and paint. She often used her artistic skills to draw in the parts that were missing from some of her photographs. In the 1970s Noel published a small book of her poetry. The poem below perhaps best describes Ruth's daily life.

MY KIND OF DAY

I sprang from my bed this morning
To greet a bright new day,
Grabbed a quick cup of coffee,
Heard what CBS had to say.

Jumped into my clothes
And scheduled my hours,
Turned on the faucet
To water my flowers.

Reached for my vacuum, but
"I'll do that after a while,"
Must mix the bread dough first
Then some negatives to refile.

I'd like to get my paints out
And fix a picture or two,
But then there's that letter
That needs replying to.

The front door flies open
And in flies my man.
Oh, for goodness sake!
I'll have to get lunch from a can.

Well, maybe things will get better
On this fine afternoon,
But don't hope too fast
Things can happen so soon.

The shirt must be mended
Before another day.
Why must some days be
Gone through this way?

Out in the darkroom
A few prints are made,
While for the tomorrow
New plans are laid.

I come out of the door,
This evening, I think;
And that's why there's dust on the sills
And dirty dishes in the sink.

Marvin wrote many articles for newspapers and magazines and was co-author with P. David Smith of two books on local history — *The Million Dollar Highway* and *Mountain Mysteries*. It has been the Gregorys' attitude that has been much more important than even their considerable achievements. They have excited and stirred the imagination of countless people who might never have thought of opening a history book. They have made the past come alive; and just like their photographs, they have done it without any embellishment and with strict attention to details. It bothered them when a writer or speaker took liberties with historic truth because, as Marvin liked to put it, "With our rich past, it simply isn't necessary to exaggerate."

Chapter 1
Men to Match My Mountains

*B*RING ME MEN TO MATCH MY MOUNTAINS,
Bring me men to match my plains,
Men with empires in their purpose
And new eras in their brains.

—from *The Coming American* by Walter Foss.

The story of the San Juans is not just the story of the land — although these mountains are some of the most exceptionally beautiful in the world. It is, perhaps more importantly, the story of the interaction of its people with the land. The inhabitants of the San Juans have not just survived in this harsh and rugged environment. Instead they have become a part of their surroundings; not trying to mold the land but rather bending their own lives to it. A life that is lived in coexistence with nature in a region such as the San Juans tempers the local inhabitants like a fire tempers steel. Most San Juan residents enjoy life to its fullest. They, by necessity, work hard and they love to play hard, too. As an early Catholic priest once wrote, "Where all is so divine, surely the spirit of man should not be merely human." (*In the San Juans*, J. J. Gibbons.)

It has always taken an extra measure of courage and strength to work in the harsh conditions of the San Juans. Perhaps the toughest of the tough has been the miner. His life was dangerous both in and out of the mine. Inside, the peril was premature explosions, falling rock, snapping cables, and bad air — just to name a few. Outside, the hazards included snow slides, freezing temperatures, wild animals (including a few of the human variety), disease and pneumonia — just to name the worst.

The original San Juan prospectors were soon followed by scores of shopkeepers who sold almost anything that you could get in the big city (except at costs that were two or three times as much) and tradesmen who could repair almost anything on the spot. Saloonkeepers, lawyers, prostitutes, freighters and a hundred other types of entrepreneurs arrived in the San Juans hoping to make their money mining the miner's pocket. These folks generally lived in town, thereby bringing a little of civilization with them. Newspapermen, sheriffs, launderers and clothiers all helped to make the rough San Juan towns just a little bit more like the place back home.

Los Piños Agency

The earliest work that was available for white men (at least legally) in the San Juans in the 1870s was at the Ute Indian agencies. The agency shown in the photograph at left served the Tabeguache Utes and was located on the Uncompahgre River near present day Colona. The post office building was made of adobe bricks, as were most of the buildings at the agency. Because of their expertise, several dozen Hispanics were brought in from what is now New Mexico to do the construction work. This was actually the second Tabeguache agency location; the first was located on Cochetopa Pass but was much too high in elevation for year-round use. The whites knew the Cochetopa to be a bad location but when the Utes got there, they refused to go further because they thought it meant they would give up more land. In fact, they were still on land they had already unknowingly given up to the whites. Los Piños II was also the site of the first post office in the San Juans. This post office carried the name "Uncompahgre" (which means hot, red water in Ute). In the photograph, Agent Joseph B. Abbott was seated in the chair and interpreter and scout Moreno was standing at the left. The Utes in the photo were all minor chiefs. Piah stood behind Agent Abbott but the others are unknown. It is interesting to see how much of the white man's clothing had already been adopted for use by the Utes.

Henry Ripley and the *Ouray Times*

Henry Ripley is the man in the middle of this early-day Ouray scene, which was shot about 1878. Henry and his brother William were the first newspaper men in Ouray, printing the initial edition of the *Ouray Times* on June 11, 1877. The Ripley's "Ouray Times - Printing Office" was directly behind Henry at a prominent spot on Ouray's Main Street. The early newspaper was extremely important to Ouray as it allowed news of its rich mines to get out to the rest of the world and, perhaps, attract some much-needed capital to the area. It took the Ripleys over two weeks to transport their heavy press, type and supplies from Cañon City to Ouray in a convoy of six wagons. The Ripleys auctioned the first paper off the press, as was the tradition in the day, and received ten dollars for it. Henry wrote with candor in his first issue: "In choosing this point as our location, we were influenced by the same motives that influenced others, chief among which is that of the almighty dollar.... The success of our enterprise means the growth and prosperity of the town." The *Ouray Times* lasted until 1886, when it went out of business, in large part, because of competition from Dave Day's infamous paper, *The Solid Muldoon*.

Camp Bird Blacksmith's Shop

Blacksmiths did a lot more than make horseshoes at a San Juan mine. They sharpened the miner's drill steel every day, and they built or repaired much of the heavy machinery at the mine or mill. A blacksmith's shop was an essential part of every mine in the San Juans — no matter how small the operation. This would have been just one corner of the large Camp Bird Mine blacksmith's shop. Pinups are on the wall behind the second man from the right. The man behind the huge anvil held the pipe with calipers, while another man used a bent rod to pull the large, red-hot pipe into position. The huge machine to the left was a trip hammer, used to mold the steel when a regular hammer wasn't large enough. The man at the door looks like a new employee since his clothes haven't even gotten dirty. This photograph was taken by Grant Marcy about 1905 during the time that he lived at the Camp Bird Mine. Unfortunately, the glass negative was cracked on the left.

A Mining Scene

Interior shots of mines were difficult to take a hundred years ago, so they were seldom seen. However, this photographer did a wonderful job of getting a good, quality shot and demonstrating many of the aspects of mining. This entire scene (which was probably shot in one of the mines near Telluride) vividly demonstrates a stope — the empty cavity that was left as the miners took out the valuable ore. The stope had a "wall" of barren rock behind the mineralized ore. The miners were both double jacking and single jacking. In "double jacking" one miner held the drill as another man swung the hammer. The double jack weighed eight pounds and the normal rate was twenty strokes a minute. With the "single jack" a miner held the drill steel in one of his hands and used a four-pound hammer in the other. Light was usually provided by candles, which can be seen here stuck into the rock wall. Miners used a wide variety of lengths in their drills. The shorter the drill, the wider the bit usually was. A stash of extra drills can be seen leaning against the wall on the right. The young man with the pick was a "mucker." Mucking was usually the first job a man got underground as it didn't require a lot of experience to pick, shovel and carry the blasted rock to the mine car. The man by the mine car was probably a foreman, checking to make sure that everything was going well on the job. The man in the front, holding a candle, may have been a geologist, examining the quality of the ore that had been previously blasted from the barren rock. In this mine the ore was so valuable that it was even being removed from below the tracks, leaving the rails hanging in the air.

Early Camp Bird Miners

This photograph of Camp Bird miners was taken at the Camp Bird boarding house in 1903 (the person writing on the negative was writing backwards and forgot to reverse the "3" so it came out an "E"). The men were of all ages, but generally they were young, since mining quickly took its toll on the men who worked in the bowels of the earth. These Camp Bird miners were not in their work clothes. The men were dressed in their Sunday best or "going to town" clothes. The very fact that they were dressed this way shows the pride that the men took in their work and in their mine. These miners were treated as human beings and not as working robots. They were some of the first miners in the nation who worked eight-hour shifts. They had plenty of leisure time. Their boardinghouse included amenities such as reading rooms, pool tables and marble vanities in the bathrooms. The men slept two to a room on white enameled beds with steel-spring mattresses. Although it was a unique idea at the time, Tom Walsh, owner of the Camp Bird, took good care of his men.

CAMP BIRD MINERS

This photograph of Camp Bird miners, taken in the late 1920s, stands in stark contrast to photographs of Camp Bird miners from around the turn of the century. By this time the Camp Bird had passed out of Tom Walsh's hands and had also been sold by the English syndicate (called the Camp Bird Ltd.) that had bought Walsh out. Presumably these men were working during the "King Lease" days. They gathered around the small boardinghouse dressed in their work clothes. They were joined by the cook and her helper, who wore white aprons. The mining engineers, dressed in their high-laced boots, stood near the doorway. This may well have been the entire work crew for the mine and mill at the time instead of the five hundred men who once worked at what was called "the great gold machine". The United States was in the Great Depression, and it was a good time just to have a job. The King Lease did well even during these hard times. The Camp Bird Mine continued to produce an average of almost a million dollars a year in ore. But somehow it just wasn't the same as the glory years, and it shows in this scene.

A MINING CREW

This crew was at the end of a tunnel (called a drift) which was probably located in the Camp Bird Mine. The men were drilling their holes for the next blast. The light was provided by two candlesticks that had been forced into the cracks at the end (face) of the tunnel. Each miner was given two or three candlesticks to use for their eight-hour shift. It was all the light they would have to enable them to do their work. The men at the back were double jacking and the man at the front was posing in a single jacking technique. A variety of tools and drills were in the area. A young boy was working on the right while the man on the left front chewed on his cigar.

Sorting Ore at the Virginius

The Virginius Mine was high up in the San Juans at over 12,000 feet elevation. It was an extremely rich mine, proving the general geological theory of the San Juans that the ore got richer the higher up in elevation that it was found. Yet the Virginius had a problem making a profit in its early days because of costs. In particular, the cost of shipping ore to the nearest smelters ran as much as $150 per ton. Shipping the ore was expensive because it had to be transported all the way to Silverton by burro or mules. The animals carried only 250 to 350 pounds at a time, usually in sacks of seventy-five to one hundred pounds. The ore was then reduced or concentrated and sent by wagon or train to a smelter in Denver or Colorado Springs. In an effort to keep these costs to a minimum, the Virginius hired a large crew of ore sorters, whose task it was to chip away all the low grade or barren rock (a job called "cobbing") before it was shipped out. "Cobbers" were usually either untrained young boys or old men who could no longer do heavy work. They were often joined by miners who were recuperating from serious injuries. In this scene there were several Chinese sorters. Chinese were seldom found working in the mines themselves. The men worked here in the sorting room of the Virginius with a large window behind them, but they also had electric lights as the days could be short in the winter. The Virginius ore would be brought to this room in ore carts and then dropped onto the grate that ran down to these men. There were no safety goggles and it was hard work but, at least, it was work!

AMERICAN NETTIE POWER HOUSE

The American Nettie Mine had its own power house to furnish electricity for its workings and mill. The power house was located alongside the Uncompahgre River, just a few hundred feet from the mill. It used water power but was, unfortunately, washed out during the same 1909 flood that did major damage to many of the buildings in Ouray. The man seated in the chair was evidently some type of watchman or operator at the power house. The large wood-burning stove would certainly have been enough to keep him and the machinery warm on even the coldest nights of winter. A myriad of early day electric dials and instruments cover the wall behind him. The mines of the San Juans were among some of the first industrial users of electricity. The very first commercial use of alternating current was at the Gold King Mine near Telluride.

CAMP BIRD CARPENTERS

It is believed that these carpenters worked at the Camp Bird Mine as only an operation that large could have afforded two full-time carpenters. Their work bench was a virtual treasure trove of early day woodworking tools. There were planes, saws, chisels, vises, drills, clamps and adzes of all types. Grant Marcy probably took the photograph about 1905. At the time almost 500 men worked at the Camp Bird Mine, mill and support facilities. The Camp Bird was larger than most of the towns or settlements in the vicinity.

ASSAYERS

These two men were assayers who examined and analyzed the ore coming out of the mine to determine its valuable components. With an assay office as extensive and complete as this, they were probably part of a large operation such as the Camp Bird Mine. Samples would be taken continually from the vein that the miners were following. This allowed the management to know whether it was worth continuing with mining that particular vein and it also gave them an idea of the best possible milling methods to use to separate the valuable minerals from the barren rock. It would further give the owners some idea of the type and amount of returns that they should receive from the smelters to which the ore was shipped. If the assayers found $200 in gold per ton and the smelters were only paying for $100, then something was definitely wrong! The ore was crushed with the machinery in the back room and placed in the cupolas that are in the middle of the photograph. The crushed ore was then mixed with chemicals and finally roasted in the oven at the left. It was a very exact science and the assayers were highly relied upon.

GOING TO WORK BY TRAM

These men look like they were going to work by tram but the scene was obviously staged about the turn of the century. The building might be the angle station at the Camp Bird Mine, at which point the tram took a hard right-hand turn. It is also possible that this tram might have been located in the vicinity of Howardsville. One of the ore buckets would have been going up while the other would be going down. Heaven only knows how the one man got up there, standing on the cable itself. It was a good way to get hurt and only goes to show that people will do anything to be included in a photograph.

MINING MEN

The mine, in the photo to the left, was identified as being in the Red Mountain District (but could have been located across the divide in Imogene Basin) and was well past its prime in the 1920s when these mining men (with the lace-up boots) showed up with potential investors. After the Silver Panic of 1893, most of the San Juan silver mines were shut down. Before the miners had left their work at this mine, they piled up the unused lumber and air pipe, and even left the ore car tipped so that the snow and rain water wouldn't collect in it. Very few of the mines totally played out of ore. It was simply a matter of the ore being too low in grade and the costs being too high. The miners usually left with the expectation that prices would soon rise and operations would then resume. For a few of the better mines, this was the case. The Idarado and the Camp Bird operated right up until recent times but they, too, have now shut down. Only a few San Juan mines still operate at present and they are being worked with minimal crews. They do not ship ore since metal prices are still too low to make much of a profit. Why give your ore away?

CARBONATE KING CREW

The miners at the right stood in front of the Carbonate King Mine in the Red Mountain District, a mine that was located further to the north than most of the rich Red Mountain mines. The remains of its surface buildings can still be seen along the Corkscrew Gulch road. The Carbonate King was a relatively small mine that worked with a small crew. The owners were trying to work a low grade ore and their costs were high. The men stood in front of the mine's boiler room, which produced steam to supply power for the pumps and winches. An old boiler had been moved outside, probably because sulfuric acid had eaten out its insides. Most of the Red Mountain ore was composed of pyrites that turned to sulfuric acid when exposed to water and air. The resulting acid made it very difficult and dangerous to work in the Red Mountain mines. The four men on the far right seemed to be the only actual miners. One of them still held a candle and the candle holder was stuck in his hat. Little mines like this always struggled for lack of money. The saying "it takes money to make money" was never more true than in the mining business.

$\mathcal{V}$IRGINIUS "MINER"?

This photograph carries the identification that it is a Virginius miner but the man is obviously not a miner. The person in the photograph looks more like a cowboy from around the turn of the century, since he is wearing a cowboy hat, chaps, bandanna, gun and holster. Perhaps he had been hired as a guard to accompany the rich Virginius ore down to Ouray. The San Juans did have its share of outlaws. Butch Cassidy and the Sundance Kid robbed the bank in Telluride. Although the Virginius never had any trouble, the Camp Bird stage was held up in 1899 by two masked bandits who took the passengers' money and several "bulbs" of gold bullion that had been placed in a locked strong box behind driver Patrick Hennesey's seat. A posse chased the robbers all the way to Utah but never caught up with the men. Later, one of the robbers, "Kid" Adams, was brought back dead by a man named Kinchen, who claimed the reward offered by the mine. Maybe the man in this photograph was hired soon thereafter by the Revenue Mine, which was mining the Virginius at the time, just to make sure that their ore wasn't stolen on the trip to Ouray. It is also possible that he was hired shortly after the turn of the century when labor troubles boiled over across the divide in Telluride, where miners were trying to unionize. The National Guard was even called in to keep the matter from literally exploding.

$\mathcal{D}$EPRESSION MINER

This miner had stopped at the entrance to his mine. It was a somewhat dangerous pose since the timbers above the entrance were broken. He was probably working the small operation by himself, just as many men did during the 1930s and 1940s. By working a mine alone and keeping costs down to a bare minimum, a man could scratch out a decent living during the depression. He carried a carbide light in his right hand and the can that held the carbide was visible in his shirt pocket. Carbide lights were used in the mines from about 1900 to 1950. When water was mixed with the carbide, it turned into acetylene. The gas was allowed to escape through a small hole in the front of the lamp which, when lit, made a small but bright flame that would give out a considerable amount of light.

Camp Bird Cobblers

Sometime between 1900 and 1910, Grant Marcy took this photo of two cobblers at work at the Camp Bird Mine. Tom Walsh, originally the sole owner of the Camp Bird, took good care of his miners. He firmly believed that if his men were treated right, they would respond in kind. He also felt that the better the men were clothed and equipped, the more able and safer they could do their work. These two men were making or repairing hobnail boots on their shoe lasts. The boots needed to be kept in good repair for the hard and wet work in the mine. The men's little tool box sat between them. Photographs of local scenery were on the shelf behind the men and the old-style crank telephone hung on the wall to the right. Several sheets of heavy leather awaited their use. There probably wasn't enough work to keep two men busy all the time so they may have done other work. Is this a cobbler and his apprentice? Perhaps a father and his son? Walsh ran the Camp Bird at a time when labor strikes and troubles were breaking out all over Colorado but there was never any trouble at the Camp Bird. Walsh urged other mine owners to treat their workers with humanity and justice. He encouraged the owners to reason and listen to the men's concerns and provide them with good food, clothing and medical attention. Tom Walsh was well-loved, not only by his men at the mine but also by the people of Ouray as a whole.

Bachelor's Home

Evidently these men were bachelors but why did they live in a structure with a sign which stated their marital status tacked over the door? One possibility was that the men were at the Bachelor Mine, named for the three single men that discovered the rich vein. Bachelors were relatively common in the San Juans, making up about half of all adult men. There was, therefore, no reason to single out these men unless there is something happening here that we don't know about. The signs look crude and temporary, as if this was done as a prank especially for the Fourth of July, 1909. There are several interesting small points in the photograph. A hatchet was stuck in the ground in front of the men. That was not the normal way to treat such a tool. The man that is second from the left had a gun in his hand. Was this to protect the men from women or was he getting ready to take a shot at the photographer? The man in the middle looks like he was bound and determined that his marital status would stay the same, while the others seemed to be taking this situation a little more in stride.

$\mathcal{U}$NDERGROUND

It was dark and dingy underground. In the old days it was also dusty. The fine dust made by the drills earned the early drilling machines the nickname "the widow maker" because the dust was breathed by the miners and sharp little pieces of rock lodged in the miner's lungs. Eventually it made it impossible for the miner to breathe which usually caused an early and painful death. The problem was solved, at least in good part, by adding water to the compressed air that fed the drills. The water produced an oily and humid mist which filled the drilling area. This photo was probably shot in the Camp Bird Mine in the early 1960s. Almost the full length of the drill was in the rock. It would then be pulled out and replaced with the longer drill on the right. Both drills had sharp carbide bits screwed on their working ends. The shorter and slightly larger drill, which started the drilling process, was also leaning against the wall to the right. A regular tangle of air and water lines could also be seen on the tunnel's floor. The vein that was being worked by this man (tentatively identified as Leo Garcia) can be seen at the upper right of the photograph.

THE DOG HOUSE

The little corner of the mine in which most of the miners ate their lunch was called the "Dog House," so named because of it size and because it usually resembled a dog house with its rough plank walls. This photo was taken in the late 1950s or early 1960s in the Camp Bird Mine. Note the nude photo at the upper middle that someone added to the sparse surroundings to lighten things up and add a little beauty. An old-fashioned crank telephone was mounted to the wall on the left of the photograph. The miners had to have their own private telephone system underground, which was continually expanded as work progressed. Several other accessories, such as gloves and liniment, were scattered around the dog house. The faces of these men, young and old, showed the strength, courage and pride that it took to work underground. The hardrock miners were certainly a special breed of men.

EXPLOSIVES

These miners of the 1960s were loading explosives into the holes they had drilled in the rock. Ron Williams is believed to be the man on the left. The boxes of explosives and detonators that the men had been using were behind and to the side of them. Obviously this wasn't old fashioned dynamite or Ron wouldn't be smoking a cigarette. Rather this was plastic explosive that was being pushed into the hole. Yet the men still used a wooden stick to lessen the chances of an accidental explosion. The vein that the hard rock miners had been following was visible in the rock above the men.

$\mathscr{F}$ORESTRY

Not all the hard and dangerous work was done underground. The man in the photo at left and others working for John or Frank Rice were cutting timber about 1920 on the Uncompahgre Plateau, probably in the vicinity of Sanborn Park. The lumber was then sent to the Rice Lumber Company in Ouray, which was some thirty or forty miles away. It was a long way but the size and quality of these ponderosa pine trees were extremely good and worth the trouble. The man in the photo below was using one of the wagon's mules to pull the huge log up a short ramp onto the wagon. With trees this size, only two of the logs made a heavy, dangerous and full load. The mule that the man was riding would then have been hitched with the other mule (perhaps even three more as shown in the photo to the left) to the front of the wagon and after that he would be ready to go to Ouray. Trees this size allowed the saw mill to make cuts of lumber that were twenty-four or thirty inches wide — sometimes even more. It took a truly virgin forest to produce such huge trees.

COWBOYS

These photographs look like scenes straight out of the movies, perhaps the epic "How the West Was Won" — which, not coincidentally, was filmed in this same general vicinity. However, these particular photographs were shot decades earlier, when Ouray County was truly in the wild west. It was branding time, and these were real cowboys doing the branding at the Henderson Ranch on Cow Creek about 1930. The photographs were taken by Marie Henderson Stankowich on her parents' ranch. (Mrs. Stankowich was a good photographer and the Gregorys have many of her images.) Ranching was always as important at the northern end of Ouray County as mining was at the southern end. There was good money to be made in the cattle business as well as in farming — as the nearby mines were full of miners who needed food and lots of it. Today, land is so expensive in most of the San Juans that ranching is no longer profitable; but, fortunately for the area, several large ranches are still run by third- or fourth-generation ranchers or have been purchased by wealthy individuals, who can still afford to operate them — even at a loss.

$\mathcal{D}$IPPING SHEEP

Once again Frank Rice took a photograph of a common scene which we don't see much of any more. This time it was dipping sheep at mid-summer. The older sheep had also been sheared. Neither the adults nor the lambs seemed to be really excited about getting into this trough since stinking chemicals had been poured from the cans that now litter the ground and sheep don't like water that much anyway. The shepherds seemed firm but kind in making sure that this job got done. Frank Rice probably ran into this operation while traveling up to the Uncompahgre Plateau to check on his logging operations. Isn't it wonderful that he took the time to catch this scene? How many times today do we take photographs of something, even everyday common events, that someone may look at fifty or sixty years from now with a sense of wonder and excitement? A chance to look back into the past is always something special.

GORDON KIMBALL HARDWARE

In 1890 Gordon Kimball advertised that his store carried hardware, stoves and tinware as well as powder and fuse. On this day a plow and harness joined a stove on display in front of his store on Ouray's Main Street board sidewalk. Note all the bottles of merchandise in the right store window and the two-man saws that hung in the left window. Gordon Kimball, a Civil War veteran, was one of Ouray's earliest residents, having moved to the town in 1878. Among many other accomplishments, Kimball helped build Ouray's first water system as well as the water systems for many other towns in the San Juans. Kimball was also extremely active in placer mining in the vicinity of Placerville and Dallas and eventually got involved with uranium mining. He died in 1924 at the age of 85 years. (This scene was copied by Ruth from a scrap book. The hinges that hold the photograph into the album can be seen at the upper corners of the photograph.)

$\mathcal{M}$OREY STORE WINDOW

The grocery store was certainly pushing "Morey" products on this particular day in the 1920s or 1930s, probably because of a very advanced and beautiful display system sent to them by the Morey Company. If one looks closely, the amphitheater's reflection can be seen at the top of the window, indicating that this shop was on the west side of Main Street in Ouray. Besides the good-looking woman drinking her coffee, there were many other signs pushing "Morey's Solitaire Coffee — Makes every meal a banquet!" Morey also produced cigars, olive oil, a large variety of spices and other items that could be seen in the window. The young clerk in the window wore a Morey hat and was evidently smoking a Morey cigar. The pay for this type of work was not high (maybe only a dollar a day) but it was much safer work than mining which paid at least three times as much.

$\mathcal{S}$TORE CLERKS

This was the inside of one of the well-known general stores in Ouray, the Cascade Grocery. Owner Joe Pricco is on the left and his partner, Mr. Faussone, is on the right. A large amount of food was being sold in bulk out of the barrels and baskets. You could buy just about anything your heart desired in a place like this about 1921 when the photo was taken. The man in the middle, who was dressed like a farmer, was either bringing in food to sell or stocking up on supplies that he couldn't grow himself. All of the men were of Italian descent. Joe Pricco's descendants now run Pricco's resturant at this same location.

Schwend-Mostyn Produce Co.

Schwend-Mostyn was a well known Ouray produce and meat market during the first part of the twentieth century. Note the way that "produce" was spelled "produse" on the awning — in fact, it looks like the "c" was recently changed to an "s". Everything had to be just right for this photograph. Mr. Schwend had on his new straw hat and suit. His five, young employees had freshly cleaned and pressed aprons. The sidewalk was washed and the large awning let down. Apples and other produce lined the window. The sign at the top of the market still stands above Duckett's Market today.

NICKEL AND SMITH

Shown here in two views taken about twenty years apart is the Nickel and Smith's butcher store (where Marvin Gregory got the job that meant that he and Ruth would move to Ouray). The first view, shown below, was taken about the turn of the century. Note that Nickel and Smith sold a lot more than meat — all kinds of vegetables were in the baskets to the right. Their store at that time included seats in front of the meat counters so that the customers could sit down while waiting for their meat orders to be filled. In those days you didn't just pick up a plastic package of whatever cut of meat you desired. You told the butcher what you wanted, right down to the exact thickness. He then took the animal's carcass out of the cooler and cut your meat to your exact specifications. The store was decorated, although somewhat sparsely, for Christmas with garlands and a paper bell.

Shortly after 1920, when the second photograph was taken, Everett Smith died, reportedly committing suicide when facing a serious illness. In this photograph Smith was in the foreground. Behind the counter from the left were Gus Nickel, Roy Laird and Louis Perotti. The woman and the boy behind Smith were unidentified. This was a typical old country store carrying just a little bit of everything. Dozens of bins lined the bottom part of the counter on the right, carrying beans and rice and many other staples. Fruits, vegetables and eggs were in the baskets to the left. The little stand in front of the meat counter carries a variety of items — all five cents per package. Pipes, cigars and tobaccos were in the case at the far left. Just about any staple that a person could want was probably somewhere to be found in this compact little store.

Ouray Firemen

This photograph was taken about 1885. The Ouray Hose Cart Team was having their annual fund-raising ball at the Dixon Hotel, which appears at the left in the photograph. Some of the town's residents and officials who were not members of the hose cart team looked on from the Dixon's front porch. Ouray also had a hook and ladder team, and the two were quite competitive. Each team had their own separate uniforms. Hose cart teams from various towns competed in races all over the San Juans. Two men could have pulled this cart downhill (except for the problem with stopping) but it would have taken most of these men to pull one of these carts up some of Ouray's steep hills. To solve that problem the company eventually purchased a fire wagon that could be pulled by either men or horses. The bugle held by the man at the far right was to warn pedestrians that the hose cart was coming. The Dixon House was Ouray's first and foremost hotel until the Beaumont Hotel was built. The Dixon's dining room was used for all kinds of meetings and dances. The building in the center of the photograph was a lodge hall, used for fraternal meetings. The building to the far right was the Presbyterian (later Catholic) church. The men of the time might well be found in any one of these three places.

ROAD-GRADING CREW

These men have just pulled up in front of a restaurant in Red Mountain Town. They may have rather been at "Washington's Place" next door but prohibition had closed the place a few years earlier. After their long and dusty day at work they surely would have preferred the saloon. They were probably part of the road-grading crew (note the blade below their wagon) that was improving the "Million Dollar Highway" from Durango to Ouray between 1921 and 1924. Although the road was being upgraded for automobiles, most of the work was done with horses and wagons. After his saloon closed, Ed Washington moved to Ouray. He was a much-beloved black man, whose main claim to fame came from his releasing a small alligator in the fish ponds near the present-day Ouray hot springs pool. The alligator grew to be seven feet long, was eventually given a mate and became a major tourist attraction in Ouray!

NEW DUMP TRUCK

The Ouray County road department was understandably proud of its new four-wheel drive dump truck. So like any parent with a new baby, they got its picture taken. This may have been both the first dump truck and the first four-wheel drive in Ouray County. It had solid rubber tires so there were no concerns about flats. To raise the bed up, the driver fixed a crank in the gear box and cranked higher and higher until the load slid out. No more hard shoveling work for the men in this photograph! The time period was evidently during World War I as the store window behind the rear of the truck was full of World War I posters and the Red Cross was also advertising for donations of clothing that could be sent overseas. The truck stopped in front of the Ouray Drug Store at the southeast corner of Main Street and Sixth Avenue in Ouray. Until prohibition in 1916 the building on the corner had been used as the Hess Saloon. In fact, this whole corner was the Hess Block. The drug store that replaced the Hess Saloon now advertised sodas, cigars and camera supplies. An attorney also had his offices above the stores. This new dump truck was important to the welfare of the entire county. The time had not yet arrived for federally supported roads. It was up to Ouray County to take care of its own. Mining was down, but tourism was exploding as the people of the United States learned of their great mobility in newfangled cars. It was important — very important — for the county's road crews to upgrade Ouray's roads so that the expected flood of tourists could start.

HATCHER BROTHERS BANK

The Thatcher brothers, who resided in Pueblo, Colorado, started banks in most of the prominent mining communities in Colorado. In Pueblo itself they started the First National Bank of Pueblo. This is an interior shot of the Thatcher Brother's Miners and Merchants Bank of Ouray. Left to right were C. T. Jordan, Assistant Cashier; E. J. Bent, Cashier; and W. W. Chapman, Bookkeeper. The sign on the left advertised that the bank could take drafts on European banks, a sure sign that Ouray was attracting many foreign visitors and investors. The bank was located at the southwest corner of the Beaumont Hotel. Banks were much simpler to run at this time, all of the work being done by the clerks shown in the photograph. The Thatcher brothers were responsible for most of the financial support for the Revenue Mine. They were originally asked to help to finance the Beaumont Hotel, but the money was raised somewhere else before they came to a decision.

$\mathcal{L}$ AST RESPECTS

This man's friends gathered to pay their last respects. Presumably he was a young man since none of these men look that old. It is very likely that these men were fellow members of one of several labor unions formed for the benefit of miners shortly after the turn of the century, and the scene may well have been in one of the rooms of the labor hall. A miner's life was so dangerous that most mining men could not obtain any type or amount of life insurance. Labor unions at least provided for a man's burial expenses in exchange for a dollar a month contribution. The dead man's friends would also "pass the hat" if the deceased left a wife or small children behind. Sometimes the result was as much as $1,000 or more to benefit the dead man's family, which in today's terms would be equal to $20,000 to $30,000. These men took care of their own.

GEORGE W. BECKWITH HEADSTONE

The American employees at the Ute agency at Los Piños II were the first to work in the San Juans. One of their numbers was also the first to die. George W. Beckwith was picked by Otto Mears to carry the mail by pack mule and saddle horse from the Cimarron agency in New Mexico Territory to the new agency at Los Piños II. About a week before Christmas in 1875, one of Beckwith's mules went lame, and he rode out to search for one of the agency's wild mustangs which he hoped to break for his own use. He roped a promising-looking mustang and tied the end of the rope to his saddle horn. Somehow both horses got tangled up in the rope with Beckwith in the center of the mess. His own horse kicked and trampled Beckwith, who died a few days later. The rocks were placed on the grave to keep wild animals from digging up the body. The fence was probably added later. (This photo was taken by Marvin Gregory in the 1960s. The lack of weeds and the addition of plastic flowers show that someone was still keeping George's grave in good shape.)

Chapter 2
Mining the Hard Rock

*T*HE FIRST WHITE SETTLERS OF THE SAN JUANS were not drawn to the mountains for the scenery. It was what was underground that brought them — gold and silver! There were so many prospectors in the San Juan Mountains in the 1870s that 125 years later the San Juan country still doesn't have as large a population as in the first decade after the discovery of precious metals. However, the prospector was soon supplanted by the miner who was responsible for the backbreaking work of actually taking the precious metals from the hard rock. The miner was hired by the capitalist who bought the mine from the prospector and was now ready to develop it. Mining took money, and lots of it, as there were pumps, winches, track, mine cars, drills and other heavy machinery to buy. The capitalist paid blacksmiths, cooks, teamsters, ore sorters and dozens of other laborers to support the miner in his work. Some of the larger mining operations employed as many as 500 men.

The rich San Juan mines were big news all over the United States. However, because of the high cost of their operations in such a steep and remote area, very few of the San Juan mines ever returned a substantial profit. Usually the capitalists made money selling stock in the mines — often for many times what the mine could have ever been expected to produce in rare metals. The miners were paid their well-earned wages. It was usually the investors who were doomed to lose money. There were exceptions, and sometimes the financial supporters really did participate in the profits of a rich strike. The Revenue, the Camp Bird and the Yankee Girl are a few examples of mines where fortunes were made. Some of these better mines returned almost one hundred-percent-a-year profit to their stockholders — at least for a while. Much more often the investor in mining stock was left holding just a pretty little stock certificate to remind him of his investment.

GUSTON AND YANKEE GIRL MINES

This sketch, which was originally published in a Ouray newspaper, shows how the buildings in the vicinity of the Guston Mine were scattered in and about the small hills and humps that were typical of the terrain near the top of Red Mountain Pass. The newspapers of the time could not reproduce photographs, so woodcuts or engravings were made from the original photographs. (This sketch, as well as the next two, are good examples of one of the sources that the Gregorys used over the years to get their images.) To the left in this scene were the actual workings of the Guston Mine. The power house had steam or smoke coming from its chimney. The freight cars of the Silverton Railroad were waiting to be loaded with ore from the company's ore sheds. Behind the ore house was the Guston shaft house. The shaft house also contained the steam-powered engines which ran the mine's winches and pumps. Uphill from the shaft house was the coal house, used to store the massive amount of coal needed for power. Behind the Guston's power house, in the distance, was the Yankee Girl Mine's tall and slender shaft house, which still stands guard over the Red Mountains. Its shaft ultimately went 1,050 feet straight down into the earth. Behind the Yankee Girl's shaft house was its power house. Notice the smoke rising from the chimney. In the far distance was Red Mountain Pass. The Yankee Girl Mine produced over ten million dollars in ore and the Guston produced close to five million. These two mines were both exceptions to the general rule and both paid high yields to their shareholders, some years paying almost one hundred percent in dividends.

GUSTON AND YANKEE GIRL GROUP OF MINES.

THE ROBINSON MINE AND BUILDINGS.

ROBINSON MINE

This sketch of the Robinson Mine shows many of the details of the cluster of buildings which were usually built around the mine shaft or tunnel proper. The power house was located to the far left and smoke could be seen coming from its chimney. Right behind the power house was the shaft house. To the right, and connected with the shaft house by an elevated ore car track, was the ore shed. The boarding house and then another ore shed were further to the right. The Robinson was located very close to the Guston Mine and both were operated in connection with each other for most of their existence. The Robinson bottomed out at 700 feet but the Guston went on down to almost 1300 feet. The Robinson was named after John Robinson, who discovered the Yankee Girl Mine. The Yankee Girl strike was so large that it was obvious to Robinson that the ore body that he had discovered might run off the standard 300 by 1500 foot mining claim. Therefore he laid out the Robinson claim on one side of the Yankee Girl and the Orphan Boy on the other. When Robinson sold the Yankee Girl Mine, he kept the Robinson claim. When it was discovered that rich Yankee Girl ore actually did run over into the Robinson claim, he struck it rich all over again.

VANDERBILT MINE

This is one of the few known photos or sketches of the Vanderbilt Mine, which was located about a half a mile south of the Yankee Girl. It was made at a time when the mine had just barely gotten under way. Notice that the lumber used on the left-hand building hasn't yet been sawed off even with the corner off the building. The logs out front could have been used for either firewood or for timbers in the mine. The sketch was made at a time when there was no railroad available to the mine and, therefore, coal was not an economic alternative. A pile of lumber used in construction was on the right. Obviously the mine's ore shed was yet to be built as ore was piled on the ground. As mining continued at the Vanderbilt, it was discovered that its ore body tied in with that of the Genessee and the operation of the two mines was eventually combined. The Genessee-Vanderbilt was a wet mine, making a drying facility a major cost cutter. Installing a dryer allowed the mine to reduce the ore's weight by over ten percent, thereby cutting its shipping costs by the same percentage. Neither the Vanderbilt nor the Genessee had extremely rich ore but they made up for quality with quantity. The mine has been worked right up to the present, and its current owners still talk of doing extensive mining to take advantage of its low grade deposits.

THE VIRGINIUS MINE

There was a general rule among San Juan prospectors that the higher in elevation the mine, the richer the ore. The Virginius Mine was one of the highest, and it was also one of the richest. It was discovered on June 28, 1876, by William B. Freeland. Because of its location at over 12,000 feet elevation on a steep talus slope, the Virginius was also one of the most dangerous and difficult to work in the San Juans. However, it produced very rich ore, averaging eight ounces of gold and one hundred-fifty ounces of silver per ton of rock and getting richer as it went down. The mine was sold in 1880 for $100,000. Because of the constant avalanche danger, the mine's buildings were constructed in such a way that avalanches were suppose to run over the top. It didn't work! A slide in December of 1883 buried twelve men, killing four; and over the years several other men were either killed or injured in slides nearby. The various tunnels and levels of the Virginius eventually totaled over three miles in length. The mine was worked from a shaft, at the location shown in this photo, until 1895 when the shaft was abandoned because of the considerable expense of using large water pumps and hoisting equipment. At that time the Virginius was accessed through the Revenue Tunnel, which was started in 1893 and reached the Virginius vein at a point almost 2,000 feet below its surface outcrop. This winter view showed the boarding house and other buildings which were located at the extreme upper level. The snow piled up so deep at the Virginius, and winter travel was so dangerous, that it was soon realized that all winter supplies needed to be brought in during the summer, and all ore taken out at the same time. The rest of the year the miners were basically trapped at the mine. Even under such conditions, the American flag was displayed proudly at the Virginius. At the time of the photo the Virginius was one of the richest silver mines in the world. It eventually produced over fifteen million dollars worth of ore.

Sneffels and the Revenue Mill

A four-horse team had stopped in front of the Sneffels post office and general store in this photo taken in the early 1900s. It was probably delivering mail and supplies to George Porter. A burro train also waited with loaded supplies on the right. John Ashenfelter's barns at the Revenue Mine were in the background on the right, while the huge sixty-stamp Revenue Mill was in the middle background. The Revenue Mill processed 500 tons of ore a day — seven days a week. The ore was reduced to forty or fifty tons of concentrates by the mill, and then shipped by wagon or mule team to the railroad in Ouray. For almost twenty years the Revenue was the largest producing mill, in terms of volume, in Ouray County. Only the Camp Bird, being a gold mine, shipped more in terms of value. The Revenue produced about fifteen million dollars in ore between 1900 and 1920, while the Camp Bird produced about twenty million dollars during the same time. Left to right in the cluster of Revenue buildings were the mill itself, the two-story bunk house for mill employees, an office building, an assay office, a blacksmith's shop, a transformer house and then a snow shed which ran quite a distance to the mine tunnel itself. Only about half of the mine's entire complex is shown in this photo with additional bunkhouses, a saw mill, compressor buildings, a machine shop, offices and several other buildings located to the right (west) of this scene. In the background is Hayden Mountain which runs for ten miles from Ouray to Red Mountain Pass. The Camp Bird Mill was located at the base of Hayden Mountain, although none of its mining activity was located there. The clouds that surround Hayden show that this scene was actually above the clouds!

THE CAMP BIRD MILL

The fabulous Camp Bird Mine was just finishing its peak years of production at the time this photograph was taken about 1920. The mine itself was actually several miles up the valley above and behind the mill. Deep snow and snow slides were constant problems for ground travel between the two locations. In 1898 the mine was connected by a 9,000-foot-long tram to this mill site. Eventually a tunnel was driven for two miles from this spot to actual mine workings in Imogene Basin. The Camp Bird's sixty-stamp mill was fed approximately 200 tons of ore a day, which produced about ten tons of gold concentrates worth $5,000 to $6,000. The value of the Camp Bird ore would be $100,000 a day in today's values! Armed guards brought each day's production to Ouray. The original Camp Bird Mill, which had been built on this same spot in 1898, was virtually destroyed by an avalanche and fire on March 17, 1906. This bigger and more efficient mill was then built. Note the avalanche defenses that were built on the slope in the upper middle of the photograph. The "fence" was meant to keep the snow from slipping, but nothing could have stopped the avalanche that hit the Camp Bird Mill in 1906. A huge slide started way up to the west on U. S. Mountain, roared down into the valley, joined up with another avalanche that had run off Hayden Mountain at the same time, took a left-hand turn and continued on down to destroy the mill. The buildings to the right in this photo included the boarding houses, reading rooms, mine and mill offices and a few houses for the families of men who were in management. In the center is the giant sixty-stamp mill, which crushed the ore to a powder which was then run over Wifley tables and amalgamation plates to catch the precious metals. At the left is the cyanide mill, which was used to capture every little bit of gold from the ore. The recovery rate of gold increased from eighty percent at the crushing mill to an average ninety-six percent recovery rate at the cyanide mill. The little building in the front left was the Camp Bird recreation and dance hall. There were additional buildings in the Camp Bird complex that are not visible in this scene.

CAMP BIRD MINE ADIT

The little light on the front of the small locomotive that pulled the ore-laden mine cars shines out of the pitch black of the Camp Bird Mine's main tunnel (adit). The photographer did a wonderful job of capturing an intangible on film — the fresh breath of air that a miner gasps as he enters back into the world above ground. The grip that winter had on the outside world (as seen in the upper middle of the photo) doesn't touch the miner who works at a constant fifty-five to fifty-eight degrees underground during winter or summer. The photograph was taken in the mid-1960s. The miners' umbilical cords were the pipes and hoses that brought water and compressed air to the pneumatic drills. Electricity for occasional light and air for ventilation were also needed. It could be lonely underground — just like the photo shows. It could also be dark. The light on the miner's hat automatically illuminated whatever he looked at, but if he turned it off it was so dark that it was as if he had no body, perhaps only a soul.

CAMP BIRD TRAM ROOM

This is a rare photograph from about 1910 of the inside of the tram room at the Upper Camp Bird Mine in Imogene Basin. The bucket on the left was loaded with 700 pounds of ore and was ready to be sent to the mill some two and a half miles downhill from the mine itself. The buckets were spaced about 450 feet apart and they traveled at a rate of about five feet per second. The man on the right may have been a mining engineer or manager since management's typical attire included the high-laced boots. The workman at the left wore typical mining attire for the time. The man in the middle looked a little like a "dude" but he may have been an oiler who wore black clothes so that stains wouldn't show. The tools in the hands of the two men to the left were used to hook and unhook the tram buckets to the cable. Trams were a very efficient way to transport ore to the mills in the rugged San Juan country. The notice on the timbers above the men warns that the employees were strictly forbidden to ride the tram. It was obviously a warning that was ignored many times as there are dozens of photographs of men riding the Camp Bird tram. Some of the San Juan mines (like the American Nettie) had their access tunnels way above the mill and the trams served as an efficient and necessary way to commute to work. However, this wasn't the case for the Camp Bird. Its tram was ridden simply for the fun of it.

$\mathscr{T}$HE GOLD CROWN MILL

The Gold Crown Mill was located alongside the Denver and Rio Grande (D&RG) Railroad's right of way, which is today called the "River Road," a northerly extension of Ouray's Oak Street. As shown in the photograph below, the mill was originally built in the late 1890s to service the Grand View Mine, which was located about halfway up the mountain behind the mill. The tramway which connected the mill to the mine can be seen at the upper left of the photo. Water from the river furnished the power for the mill. However, there was not nearly enough ore produced in the area to keep the mill running. The mill was partially destroyed by fire but was rebuilt about 1920 by the Gold Crown Mining and Milling Company. It is shown in the upper right photograph at approximately this time. Ore was then obtained from the Two Kids Mine across the river on the cliffs to the east of the present day hot springs swimming pool. Again, there was not enough ore to keep the mill operating. A few years later the mill was again repaired and remodeled by Frank Henn. Considerable money was spent on the project and electric power replaced the water power. A few test runs were made, but before the mill was ever put into operation again it was completely destroyed by fire. The lower right photo shows just how complete the fire was in its destruction. The area to the front of the mill was part of the Uncompahgre River flood plain. The D&RG Railroad elevated its tracks to avoid the flood danger, making a ramp necessary to get to the mill. After the second fire the mill was never rebuilt. Now only the concrete foundation remains.

HERCULES MINE

The No. 2 Tunnel of the Hercules Mine is shown in this photo (which Ruth Gregory copied from a postcard). The Hercules' crew had a wonderful view of the town of Silverton, Colorado. Silverton's baseball field showed up well in the large, flat area below the mine. The waste dump for the mine was below the track that ran out on the timbers. Sometimes the miners might be following a rich vein that was only a few inches wide, yet the valueless rock still had to be blasted wide enough to create a tunnel that could accommodate the miners and their equipment. This width was usually about three feet. The valueless debris that was created was called "country rock" and it was placed on the waste dump. The track that curved to the left in this scene went to the mine's storage bins where the ore was held until it was shipped. Ore is defined as rock which contains enough valuable minerals to make it profitable to extract and sell.

SILVER LEDGE MINE

The Silver Ledge Mine (in the lower right of the photograph) was located just on the southern side of Red Mountain Pass. The little settlement of Chattanooga could be seen in the valley below. It was a steep climb from the valley to the top of the pass, just barely passable by the Silverton Railroad when the famous Chattanooga loop was built in 1888. Bear Mountain was visible in the upper left-hand corner of the photograph. It was named for the image (formed by the trees) of a bear holding a honey comb in its paws. The Silver Ledge Mine was discovered in 1878. It took a while before its owners realized that it carried a very rich silver ore. In 1883, when the Red Mountain District was just coming into prominence, the Silver Ledge took the lead over all other local mines. Unfortunately, its ore contained a lot of zinc which was hard to process at the smelters. So the Silver Ledge was almost forgotten for a decade. It did well during the 1880s but the other Red Mountain mines did much better. It was about 1890, at the end of the Red Mountain Mining District's heyday, that the Silver Ledge came back into prominence. Then, in 1892, the shaft house caught fire, igniting forty pounds of dynamite in the nearby powder house and blowing most of the mine's surface buildings into small pieces. The Silver Ledge again rebounded, this time building a mill in the Chattanooga Valley that could, for the first time anywhere, process zinc ore economically. The mine continued to operate until its mill was totally destroyed by fire in 1919.

THE ENTERPRISE MINE

This mine has been identified as the Intersection Mine, but it is believed to be the Enterprise Mine, which was the largest mine in the vicinity of Rico, Colorado. It was located on a hillside just up from the mill and the town of Rico. The Enterprise was discovered in 1868 and continued to amaze mining men as one new, rich discovery seemed to keep coming after another. Until the arrival of the Rio Grande Southern (RGS) Railroad, most of Rico's supplies were brought in by oxen. The mine was still using oxen to pull its wagons at the time of this photograph. Since they could pull extremely heavy loads, oxen were quite commonly used in the early days of mining activity in the San Juans. They were more dependable and stronger than mules or horses but they were also much slower. In this photo they were carrying what looks to be railroad ties, perhaps to prepare for the arrival of the construction crews of the RGS Railroad. There were more oxen that can be seen through the trees pulling wagons piled high with ties over the road in the background. It is also possible that these could have been mine timbers or even firewood. Several men were building a new house at the left center of this photo. There were over fifty men at work on the surface doing one job or another on this particular day.

$\mathcal{T}$HE ENTERPRISE MILL

The Enterprise Mill at Rico, Colorado, was a huge operation, greatly responsible for the employment of a large part of the population of the town. A good example of some of the work going on around a mill was shown in this photograph which was taken shortly after the turn of the century. On the hillside was a pack train which carried timbers. Firewood or more timbers were on the ground in front of them. Tram towers came down from the mine at the right and railroad tracks came in from the same direction. Avalanche defenses can be seen on the hillside. The Enterprise Mill itself was in the foreground. It had already churned out tons of tailings which filled the large tailings pond in the foreground. This type of tailings pond is now a large part of the environmental cleanup mandated by the federal government.

Silver Link Mine

The Silver Link Mine may have been located in one of the steepest and most inaccessible locations in all of the San Juans, as it was situated up on the high cliffs at the very beginning of the present day Engineer jeep road. Three of its miners can be seen here. Only the mine track ran out to the man on the right, and then it just dropped off into space. Snow covered the backside of the building and the smokestack on the left was raised an extra ten feet or so to keep it from being totally buried during heavy snows. The mine's only outside structure was built under a steep cliff in the hope that an avalanche would pass over the top of it. The Silver Link was located at 10,500 feet and followed a huge vein that was sometimes as much as twenty-feet wide. The Silver Link doesn't look like much of a mine in this scene, mainly because there wasn't any more room for anything to be built on the outside, but it had over 2,200 feet of drifts (tunnels). Hand-picked ore from the mine contained up to 300 ounces of silver per ton and assayed at thirty percent copper. The mine was extensively developed in the 1880s and operated well into the twentieth century.

ℳINING ABOVE TIMBERLINE

This mine was identified as being located at Red Mountain or Brown Mountain. However, it looks like it could be the area around the Virginius or even up on Engineer Mountain. It always takes some detective work to figure out exactly where an unidentified scene was located. At any rate, the men were working way above timberline in what was called scree rock (loose, broken rock). They were mining from a shaft or tunnel located at the left. They had been stacking bags of their high-grade ore for shipment. The ore was being shipped out on burros. The men behind the ore sacks seemed to be loading the sacks for shipment, while the men at the top were evidently in the process of building some type of structure for the mine. In between was a log frame that seemed to be the start of what eventually would become an ore chute. There was lumber next to the men at the top, as well as near the burros in the middle of the photo. Probably the lumber was brought up by these same burros, some of which were wandering on the hillside behind the mine. Now it was time for the burros to carry the ore back to town. The photographer probably caught this particular mine somewhat early in its existence when serious mining operations were just getting started.

WINTER AT THE HIDDEN TREASURE

The winter snows could build up quite deep at the Hidden Treasure Mine, located slightly above the main complex of the Upper Camp Bird Mine. Sometimes snow would totally cover the local cabins to a depth of four or five feet. This photograph was taken in the spring of 1922 by Minnie McCullough. The Hidden Treasure was kept by Tom Walsh when he sold the Camp Bird Mine to an English syndicate for $5.2 million. He always thought he might strike it rich all over again at this mine. It has been passed down through the Walsh family all the way to present with each generation still believing it to be a potentially rich and profitable property. Several lessees reported its ore to be composed of mainly low grade minerals. In this photo the mine was evidently being worked but only on a very small scale. It looked like winter was almost over and Imogene Basin was starting to thaw. (In fact, this photograph could well have been made in June.) In the background was what is called a "rock glacier." Thousands of years ago a glacier shrank until it melted entirely at this point, leaving a rock formation that looks almost liquid. The Camp Bird No.1 level was at the top of this particular formation and the No. 2 level was at the bottom. The covered ore trestle of the Camp Bird No.3 level was in the dip to the left. Most of the Upper Camp Bird buildings were hidden behind the ridge that the two little log cabins were built on.

TOMBOY MINE

Within the photos to the left are two mines. The Tomboy Mine (to the right in each) and Japan Mine (to the left in each) were located in Tomboy Basin, just a short distance from the town of Telluride. These two photos were basically the same except the first was taken in the winter and the second was photographed in the summer. Because of the steep and dangerous trail, the mines were all but totally isolated for most of the winter. Imogene Pass would be at the far upper left in both scenes and the road to Telluride at the right; but both roads were often impassable to all but foot travel in the winter. Avalanches were a constant danger and there were many winter travelers killed along these roads. The winter scene, taken January 17, 1925, shows just how solitary it was in Tomboy Basin at 11,500 feet in the middle of winter. Although isolated, the inhabitants of the basin had plenty to do. Tomboy was a company town and the valley was filled with mine buildings, the sixty stamp mill (here spewing out smoke), livery stables, a school, homes, shops, a three-story boarding house and even several tennis courts, a theater and a bowling alley. The summer scene demonstrates just how rough the terrain was in the basin. The Japan Mine did well but the Tomboy Mine was spectacular. The Tomboy was discovered in 1880 and prospered into one of the richest mines in the United States. It was purchased by the Rothschilds of London in 1897 for $2 million. About the turn of the century the Tomboy Mine was the scene of major labor troubles, some of which ended with loss of life. Winter life in Savage Basin was vividly described by Harriet Bacus in her book *Tomboy Bride*. She was a newlywed and reported a never-ending battle against the cold and snow. Avalanches roared down into the basin and sometimes snowdrifts built up to twenty feet deep. She had to depend on supplies being delivered by the occasional pack trains that were coming up to take the ore down to Telluride. Usually she bought six months of supplies at a time. Mrs. Bacus even reported that the pack rats took her silverware from her drawers during the night and rearranged them on the floor. The Tomboy Mine closed in 1927 and most of its machinery was used for scrap metal during World War II. The Idarado Mining Company continued to work the Tomboy's ore through underground access until 1979.

THE MICKY BREENE

This mine, which is known to most locals as the Micky Breene, was actually named the Michael Breene or the Mountain Monarch. The two mines were side by side and little attention seems to have been paid as to which was which. Both claims were some of the earliest in the San Juans — located in 1874 by Milton W. Cline, who later became the first mayor of Ouray. The Micky Breene and Mountain Monarch have been worked off and on ever since, most recently in the 1980s; and they have produced a lot of good ore. However, expenses have always been high because of their remote location. Even though a small mill was built to help concentrate the metals before shipment, costs were still too high. Despite rich ore, the mine usually did little more than break even. A fair portion of the Mountain Monarch Mine still exists, so it is a favorite stop on the local Engineer Pass jeep tours. In the background of the photo at the left is an unnamed but major avalanche that always covers the road and the Uncompahgre to some depth even in the early summer, usually not melting totally, even at the end of the summer. The photo below shows a close up of some of the buildings and trestles. The mine looks abandoned but may not have been. Perhaps the woman and girl were cooks there at the time or were they merely posing for the photographer?

$\mathcal{T}$HE OLD HUNDRED MILL

The Old Hundred Mill was located about a mile up Cunningham Gulch from Howardsville and looked pretty deserted on this winter day. The Green Mountain Mill was also visible in the background, but it appears very blurry because of the dense smoke coming from its coal-fired boilers. A scattering of residences and other buildings surrounded the mill. The Green Mountain Mine was one of the oldest claims in the San Juans and it and the Old One Hundred Mine also ranked among the richest. Both mines were connected by tramways to their mills, as were several other mills and mining operations in Cunnigham Gulch. The Old One Hundred Mine was a steep quarter of a mile from its mill, while the Green Mountain tram ran for over a mile up a rather gentle but dangerous valley. The stamp mills pulverized the ore with huge pestles (stamps), which were pushed up by a cam and came crashing down with great force. Then the rich minerals could be concentrated in other processes to remove the barren rock. (Ruth and her mother spent a winter at the Green Mountain Mill when Ruth was but a little girl.)

JOKER TUNNEL

The Joker Tunnel was not actually a mine; rather it was an access tunnel. Its purpose was to strike the rich ore of the Yankee Girl, Guston, Gennesse and other prosperous Red Mountain mines at a point well down into their workings. It was hoped that such a feat would solve many of the problems that had caused the Red Mountain mines to close. The tunnel would drain by gravity the water that in the past had to be pumped hundreds of feet to the surface. It would also allow the ore to be brought out by ore cars rather than having to be hoisted in buckets to the surface. The Joker Tunnel was right next to the Silverton Railroad's tracks so shipping costs for its ore were minimal. The Joker was also able to have coal shipped in on the railroad at a minimal cost. The project worked, except the developers didn't realize that most of the Red Mountain mines were down to mining only a low grade ore when they quit operation. Unfortunately, the ore continued to lose value as the Joker Tunnel worked these great old mines to deeper levels. A small community grew up around the Joker Tunnel in the early twentieth century. This photograph was taken about 1910 or 1915 when the main operation was about to close down. The tunnel showed some sporadic use on into the 1940s. The building on the far right was a residence and office. The power house (with the large smoke stack) was to the left. Next to the power house was the boarding house and kitchen. Another boarding house, which still stands today directly beside U. S. Highway 550, stood to the left of the kitchen. To the far left were the carpenter and blacksmith shops that stood beside the entrance to the tunnel.

SILVER LAKE MINE

This photograph reminds one of a current day Bev Doolittle painting, but it is an actual photograph of Silver Lake taken about the turn of the century. There were no roads to the mines located at Silver Lake, so all supplies were brought in from Arrastra Gulch by two aerial tramways. All of the rich ore from the mines in the area was brought out the same way. Many of the miners and mill workers would ride the tram back to work after visiting their families or the bars and brothels in nearby Silverton. Even the tramways were not safe from the snow slides; the two Silver Lake trams were hit some six times in twenty years. The mine and mill in this scene is the Royal Tiger. The Iowa was a quarter mile away, and the Silver Lake Mine was across the lake. The Iowa-Tiger and Silver Lake were connected by a cableway that stretched across the lake. Today this spot can only be reached by a steep hike over a narrow trail, but the scenery is well worth the effort. Legend has it that local miners hid high grade ore around the edges of Silver Lake, pieces of which still wait for some discerning visitor to find today.

ᎶOLD PRINCE MILL

The one hundred stamp Gold Prince Mill was at the terminus of the Silverton Northern Railroad —
one of Otto Mears' later ventures, as construction on the railroad wasn't even started until 1896. The route
to Animas Forks was a steep grade for Otto Mears' little narrow gauge train — so steep (seven to seven
and a half percent grades) that on the portion of track from Eureka to Animas Forks, the locomotive had
to push the cars up the tracks because the car's brakes would not have held them on such a steep grade if a
coupling broke. On the way down, the locomotive would proceed the cars. Even with all the precautions,
the Silverton Northern would not attempt to haul more than three cars at a time. The railroad was started
at a time that was not good for mining in most of the San Juans, but the little line did succeed. The Silver
Panic of 1893 had shut down many of the San Juan mines; however, the Gold Prince, as the name implies,
mined gold — not silver. The Gold Prince was located at 12,200 feet in elevation at the head of Placer
Gulch. A two-mile tram connected the mine with the mill. Some of the Silverton Northern's freight cars
(most marked D&RG) are visible in front of the mill. The Gold Prince Mill, when built in 1907, was the
largest stamp mill in Colorado and was one of the first large mills to be built of structural steel. Each of its
one hundred stamps weighed about 750 pounds and they would fall at a rate of up to one hundred drops
a minute, pulverizing a total of over 300 tons of ore a day. After ten years the mill was dismantled and
moved with some of its equipment and structure parts to Eureka, Colorado, to be used in the Sunnyside
Mill. Now only the concrete foundation remains. It is still impressive.

*G*OLD KING MILL

The Gold King Mill was captured on film at Gladstone in 1905. The extremely rich Gold King Mine was discovered in 1887 and only recently shut down after being operated for a long time by the Sunnyside Mine. The Silverton, Gladstone and Northerly (SG&N) Railroad was built to serve the Sunnyside Mill and the adjacent Mogul Mill. The little town of Gladstone developed around the mill and eventually grew to a population of almost 200 people. The SG&N railroad was one of the few lines in the San Juans that Otto Mears did not actually build. However, soon after the railroad was built in 1907, the SG&N was leased and then purchased by the Silverton Northern which Otto Mears did build. At the extreme left of the photograph are large wooden chutes for delivering coal to the mill's boilers. Freight cars were scattered all over the Gold King's yard on this particular day, either delivering supplies or waiting to be loaded with ore concentrates. The Gold King's tram entered the mill about the point of the top of the smokestacks. Miners were allowed to ride the two-mile Gold King tram to the upper workings, and they often did so. The mountain in the background is Storm Peak.

GRIZZLY BEAR

The Grizzly Bear Mine was one of Ouray County's earliest and richest mines, but it was located in a hard to reach location which was several miles up Bear Creek. There never was a railroad, tram or even a wagon road built to the mine. All of the ore went out by pack trains which made the Grizzly Bear very expensive to operate. Although it was located in 1875, the Grizzly Bear didn't reach its peak production until around 1890. Much of its ore was extremely rich in silver and, even using only burros and mules, the mine managed to ship over $650,000 worth of ore before shutting down. A small town rose up in the vicinity of the mine. Its 1900 census population was officially listed at twenty-four. The Grizzly Bear is one of the few mines in the central San Juans still being operated at present. A 6,000 foot tunnel was recently run to the mine from the Amphitheater near Ouray, and much of the old ore workings were struck at a lower level. No ore is being shipped at present as the mine's owners are waiting for metal prices to go up. In this photograph, the mine's boarding house was up the hill to the left. The mine itself was at the far right of the photograph, connected to the mine's buildings at the left with the large wooden trestle. The owner, George Hurlburt, as a publicity stunt had invited many of Ouray's residents to visit the mine for a picnic. Several of the mine's ore cars are on the trestle this "special" day as well as several men, at least four women, and a horse.

$\mathscr{S}$ IEBURG TUNNEL

The Sieburg Tunnel was not a mine but rather an access tunnel driven into Gold Hill, just north of, but a thousand feet higher in elevation than the city of Ouray. (Ouray can be seen in the background of the photograph at the left.) The tunnel was driven into the mountain for about 2,000 feet to access the rich American Nettie workings at a lower level. The American Nettie was a gold mine. It was discovered shortly before the price of silver fell. Part of the boarding house, seen in the photo below, can still be seen today. The buildings of this mine literally clung to the hillside a thousand feet above the valley floor; yet women, children and dogs were present. Even the boarding house outhouse hung over the side of the cliff! Some of the men who worked at the mine walked from Ouray every day, choosing the long steep hike so that they could be with their families at night.

AMERICAN NETTIE MILL AND TRAM

The American Nettie Mine probably saved the City of Ouray from becoming a ghost town in 1893, when the price of silver fell drastically during the Silver Panic which occurred when price stabilization measures for silver were removed. The San Juan mines produced mainly silver and lots of it. But when silver prices fell from $1.25 to sixty cents almost overnight, mines shut down throughout the San Juans. Luckily, the American Nettie's extensive gold deposits had been recognized in the late 1880s. Its claims spread up and down the cliffs to the northeast of Ouray. The mine ultimately produced over two million dollars in ore, which would be worth twenty times that much today. Although a gold mine, the American Nettie had a form of ruby silver that was so red that the miners used to say that their drills were bleeding when they passed through it. The mine was located 1,800 feet above the valley floor, making necessary the tram that is seen in the photograph below. The mill, which is seen in the photo to the right, was built in the valley below the tram and it still stands today. The tram's cable hung across the valley until the 1960s when it was struck by an airplane, killing all of the plane's occupants. The American Nettie was one of the first mines in the world to use electricity. Its generating plant was located close to the mill. It used water from the Uncompahgre to power its turbine.

𝒯HE TREASURY TUNNEL

The Hammond Tunnel (later called the Treasury Tunnel) was started in 1896. The plan was to work the old mines located between Telluride and Red Mountain at lower levels and hopefully make a few new strikes along the way. A 2,000 foot railroad spur was run from across the valley. Mining took place through the tunnel for about ten years before it shut down. It then operated off and on until taken over by the San Juan Metals Company in the 1930s. In 1939 several companies, which eventually became the Idarado Mine, took over operations. For the next forty years the Idarado was the foremost mining operation in the San Juans and often the number one gold producer in the United States. The Idarado also produced large amounts of silver, lead, zinc, copper and other metals. Eventually the Idarado took control of over eighty miles of interconnected tunnels. The mine closed in 1979. Just as in the closure of all the other San Juan mines, everyone felt that the mine would soon reopen. It has now been almost two decades, and a skeleton crew still maintains the Idarado Mine — just waiting for the sharp rise in metals prices that would mean the reopening of what was once one of the foremost mines in the United States. If it were to reopen there would be many problems to solve. Where would the ore be milled? Where would tailings or other byproducts be stored? How would ore be shipped? What about other environmental factors since the San Juans are now one of the foremost recreational areas in the West? These questions remain unanswered for now.

Chapter 8
Building a Future

THE STOREKEEPERS AND TRADESMEN who followed the prospector and the miner into the San Juans needed a place to set up their business establishments so they could sell their wares and ply their trade. So towns were built almost as fast as the prospectors could push their small discovery cuts into the mountains. Just like the mining capitalists made money selling stock in their mines to investors, so did the town builder make his money selling lots to potential businessmen and homeowners. Towns sprang up "in some of the darndest places" — some so high and exposed to the elements that they were obviously doomed to failure from the start. Others, which were built at the edge of the mountains or in large, broad valleys, tended to grow and prosper. In the 1880s and 1890s, Silverton and Ouray grew so fast that they were among the top ten largest communities in Colorado. Telluride and Durango both prospered just a little later, and Rico also grew to quite a large size during the 1890s.

All of the San Juan towns followed approximately the same cycle. Originally they were a crude collection of rough log cabins built from trees that were usually cut right on the spot. The idea was only to protect the new arrivals from the harsh winter elements and style wasn't a major consideration. A little later in the town's life cycle a sawmill would be established and rough-sawn cabins were built. Still later more finished siding might cover the rough logs or timbers. As soon as a real element of stability struck (usually a decade or so after the town's founding), brick plants would be built. Fire danger was greatly eliminated by the brick buildings, and the town took on a look of much greater permanence. If the local mines played out, however, a town could disappear as quickly as it had been built — sometimes literally overnight — as buildings were either torn down for their materials or moved to new locations.

OURAY, 1877

This pen and ink drawing is the earliest known representation of the settlement of Ouray. The artist took the liberty to make Ouray look a little more developed than was actually the case in the last part of 1877. Photos from the next year, for example, show tree stumps everywhere and the streets to be in very poor condition. This drawing points out clearly that the commercial district along Main Street was really the only area of any substance in the new town. The rest of the structures in the small settlement were basically just log cabins. The town's thirteen- by twenty-foot American flag, which had been made that year for the Fourth of July festivities, was proudly displayed on the fifty-foot flag pole at the center of town.

TOWN OF OURAY, CIRCA 1880

Many of the buildings that are seen in this photograph are the original prospectors' log cabins that were built in the summer of 1876, a year after Ouray was "officially" discovered. Actually, whites had been in the valley for at least fifteen years prior to that time; and, of course, the Ute Indians had visited the Ouray amphitheater for centuries. Before 1876 the lovely bowl was heavily forested. Ouray had a working sawmill in 1877, and the quick result was a town full of stumps! The frame buildings in this photo were mainly commercial establishments and mostly located on Ouray's Main Street. A few are even two-story. Ouray had a very "unsteady" look, since it really wasn't known at this time whether the new settlement would last or would become abandoned on a moments' notice when the local mines played out or if gold and silver prices fell. It was most probably spring (late April or early May) since a few deep snowdrifts remain in the foreground. The sunny south-facing slopes are bare of snow. The local residents had built a great number of log cabin homes on Oak Street, to the west (left) of the Uncompahgre River. Oak Street is still a favorite part of Ouray because of the dramatic views of the amphitheater and the rest of the town. No one knows the identity of the boy in the photo, perhaps the son of the unknown photographer.

OURAY, 1885

Ouray's Main Street was pretty well deserted in the scene below, which was photographed between Fifth Avenue and Sixth Avenue. From the time of Ouray's original settlement, the west side of Main Street has been the most popular side of the street. The reason is unknown, but it is the downhill side and better allows for basements. It also seems that, for some reason, more customers walk on the west side. The commercial buildings in this photograph are (from the left) the Capitol Saloon, once one of Ouray's most popular; the original City Hall, with a hose cart out front; Talcott's; the Dutton Saloon; and a hardware store that also sold powder and mining supplies. The fifty-foot-high flag pole was still in the middle of the intersection of Main and Sixth Avenue. In this view it is easy to see that it was built in two pieces. The speakers' stand had not yet been built. There was no Corner Saloon (the present Citizens State Bank building) at the corner of Main and Sixth Avenue at the time of this photograph, so the photo was probably taken in the early half of the 1880s.

The scene above was shot at about the same time but looking in the other direction. The Beaumont Hotel was later built at the far end of the left (east) side of this block in 1886. In the foreground on the left can be seen H. G. Corson's men's furnishings shop which handled boots and shoes. His establishment evidently included a barber shop as evidenced by the barber pole out front. The east side of the street also had several drug stores. Way down and across Fifth Avenue was the two-story Morris Kirkpatrick Furniture Store, which was built in 1882. The building on the right-hand side of the street (with the crude flagpole on top) was Ouray's early day city hall. Near the end of this block on the right were a barbershop, a jewelry store and, at the very end, the Bucket of Blood Saloon. Across Fifth Avenue on the east side of Main, was the white two-story Wright Building — the forerunner of the Wright Opera House. It was built in 1881 and was the largest office building in Ouray at the time with twenty-one offices. The basement contained a saloon. In the middle of the photograph was the city's ever-present flagpole. Note the pegs that had been inserted for steps. Someone has also posted some kind of circular on the pole, perhaps for the circus?

OURAY, CIRCA 1910

L. C. McClure climbed high on the cliffs to the west of Ouray to take this photograph for promotional purposes for the Denver and Rio Grande (D&RG) Railroad. Unfortunately the print was torn in the upper right quadrant. The Ouray depot is in the foreground. Several men sat near the corner of the D&RG's freight platform awaiting the arrival of the daily train. The line of box cars behind the depot also wait to be towed away. To the left of the depot was a short spur than ran to the Munn Brothers Sampling Works, a part of which can be seen in the trees. Past that was the Beaumont Sampling Works, the Rice Lumber Company and the Revenue Mine's power station. The pedestrian bridge immediately to the left of the depot took passengers up Eighth Avenue through the town's red-light district. Most of the buildings directly on the other side of the Uncompahgre River were either saloons or houses of prostitution, so it was preferred for the train passengers to go south to the full-size bridge a block away on Seventh Avenue. Further up Eighth Avenue were John Ashenfelter's barns and stables for his huge freighting outfit. The large billboard next to the river advertised "Borden's - Columbian - Real Roasted Cream." Most of the prominent brick buildings had been built in Ouray by this time, so the photograph probably dated from about 1910. Note that the highway didn't go out of town to the south like it does at present. Before 1920 it passed through the present highway department grounds on the Camp Bird Road and then continued on to the south.

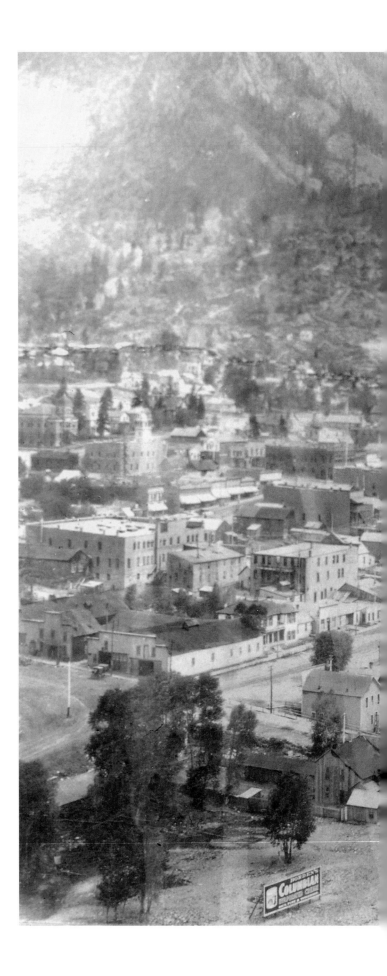

Louis King's Shop, Ouray

Louis King's Carriage Shop and Livery Stable was showing its age in this photograph taken about 1920, but his building actually stood into the 1980s when Ouray's community center was built. The clock on the Ouray City Hall identifies the time as 9:45. Down the street was an office, Brumfield's Photo Studio, Dr. Rowan's office, a restaurant, and across Main Street Citizen's State Bank (originally the Corner Saloon). Ouray's famous City Hall was originally built in 1900 and was patterned after Philadelphia's Independence Hall. The second floor, the tower, the gold-leaf dome and a large brass bell were all gifts to the citizens of Ouray from Thomas Walsh, owner of the fabulously rich Camp Bird Mine. The top floor housed the town's library — also a gift from Walsh. The building was destroyed by fire in 1950 and the library (then valued at $50,000) was also totally ruined. There was no insurance but city hall was rebuilt in "adobe" form that year with volunteer labor and then reconstructed in 1988 to nearly its original appearance. This time the money came from hundreds of citizens and tourists who just love Ouray.

ᏢOWER DAM & PEST HOUSE, OURAY

The dam across the Uncompahgre River that is shown in this photo was originally created to use water to power several of the town's early smelters. The water was carried in the wooden flume to the left of the dam. Later, a pipeline was laid into Box Canyon to bring water to the town's original hydroelectric plant. Because the Box Canyon water contained many fine particles from mill tailings that were destroying the electric plant's Pelton Wheel, the intake was soon changed to another dam located several miles to the south of Ouray on the Uncompahgre River. The large steel pipeline that connected the two can be seen in the upper right of the photo. The little house that is in the far background on the hill has an interesting history. It was built by Fred Smith, a prospector who bragged so much about his "rich" finds that he was dubbed "Millionaire Smith." After Smith died, his family moved away and the cabin stood abandoned. Smith's cabin was often used for quarantined patients and took on the name of the pest (or pestilence) house. When a full-scale small pox epidemic hit Ouray, "Shorty" King (every one said the nickname fit) took over watching the sick. Once a day Dr. Rowan would check in on the patients but many died. After the epidemic passed, the building was burned in order to prevent anyone from contracting the disease through contact with the cabin.

℘ORTLAND

Of all the scheming, get-rich plans for new towns in the San Juans, Portland probably was the best planned and yet the largest failure. It was the brainchild of Dave Day, Ouray's infamous newspaper publisher. Day was a friend of David Moffat, president of the Denver and Rio Grande (D&RG) Railroad. For years Day badgered Moffat to build his railroad on into Ouray. In 1886 it looked like the branch to Ouray would be built in the near future, but Day believed that the railroad couldn't make the steep grades of the last few miles into Ouray. So Day planned a town a little to the north of Ouray on the last large flat area before the steep grade. Day put every last penny he had into the project and touted its glowing future in every week's edition of the *Solid Muldoon*. However Ouray's citizens rallied and convinced Moffat to build into their city by using a route on the other side of the river. Day had already sold many lots in the new town of Portland and several businesses had been established in anticipation of the railroad's arrival. Under the new plan the railroad wouldn't even pass through the town, much less terminate its branch at Portland. The people of Portland were furious. The people of Ouray were ready to run Day out of town. Day was boycotted and his very profitable newspaper quickly went downhill, eventually forcing Day to move his operation to Durango.

$\mathcal{M}$AIN STREET, SILVERTON

This scene of Silverton's Main Street was taken about 1885. (It was made from a negative loaned to Ruth by John Abrams of Texas. Mr. Abrams' father was one of the discoverers of the famous National Belle Mine in the Red Mountain Mining District.) The scene was looking east. The Grand Hotel (now called the Grand Imperial) was on the left. The building was started in 1882 and it originally housed not only the hotel but also the county offices, a saloon, a hardware store and many other establishments. The sign on the side read "Mining Industrial Bureau." Many wagon tracks still remained to mark Main Street after a heavy summer rain but the street looks almost deserted.

SILVERTON

The snow had piled up to ten feet deep in Silverton in March of 1909. The scene below seems to be in front of the Grand Imperial Hotel and the large, fancy clock advertised for watch repairs and sales at a jeweler's (possibly Rose's) establishment. Hank's Place saloon advertised that it served Faust beer. The snow can build up quite deep in Silverton in the winter but this must have been close to a record. Since all this snow happened at a time before snow plows or snow blowers, all ten feet of snow must have been shoveled by hand to clear the streets and sidewalks.

$\mathcal{S}$ILVERTON

The photograph above was taken of Silverton about 1882 or 1883. It must have been the end of summer based on the lack of snow in the nearby mountains. Someone had planted a nice stand of evergreens in front of the meat market. Some of the other businesses included in the photograph are a bakery, a restaurant and a hardware store. On the other side of the street was a freight and forwarding service which would divide up shipments coming in on the train and send them along to the individual mines. Silverton was founded in 1874 and the town grew quickly. At the time of this photo it was at its prime with a population of almost 5,000. This made it one of the largest towns in Colorado. Most of these men were probably coming to town to get supplies or to make early morning deliveries. Sultan Mountain formed a beautiful backdrop for the town.

RIDGWAY

Ridgway was established in March of 1890 as the terminus of the new Rio Grande Southern (RGS) Railroad. It was originally called Magentie, then McGinty, Jordan and Dallas Junction. Finally, the name was changed to Ridgway in honor of R. M. Ridgway. Streets running east-west in Ridgway were named after the town's founders and their male relatives. Those streets running north-south were named after their female relatives. As early as November of 1890, many of the buildings shown here had already been constructed. The Mentone Hotel was the large building with gables behind the first street near the center of the photo. The large building to the right was the Mears Building. The town hall was the white building at the center. Left to right were a general store, a millenary, and the offices of the *Ridgway Herald*. The photograph was probably taken about 1910. Several of the work cars that were used for repairs and other construction work along the RGS tracks are in the foreground. The RGS Railroad was started in 1890 with construction beginning at the same time on both ends of the line (Durango and Ridgway). The construction crews met at a point eleven miles south of Rico in December of 1891.

CHATTANOOGA

In the above scene (taken from a stereo card) the settlement of Chattanooga was in the midst of the winter snows. Almost forty cabins or houses were visible in the photograph. Chattanooga was at the end of a long, gentle valley that ran from Silverton to the base of Red Mountain, so it exploded with activity when rich silver discoveries were found on up the mountain. The town's roads ran north and south at the time and the Silverton Railroad had yet to arrive. The photo was taken before 1888 when a snow slide wiped out most of the town. The town was then rebuilt with its few remaining streets being oriented east and west. The settlement was founded under the name "Sweetville" in 1883, but its name had been changed to Chattanooga by the end of the year. The town was a supply point for the booming Red Mountain Mining District. A month after its founding, Sweetville already contained seventy-five structures in some stage of construction, and its population was over 300. Supplies could be brought to this point by wagon and then transferred to mules or burros for transport on up the mountain. After the Silverton Railroad was constructed through the town in 1888, the supplies no longer needed to be transferred, and Chattanooga's population went downhill quickly. The snow slide finished it off. Then, to add insult to injury, what was left of the town burned a few years later.

CONGRESS TOWN

The Congress Mine was discovered in July of 1881 on the south side of Red Mountain Pass, making it one of the first of the large Red Mountain mines. The original owners did not realize the value of their discovery until about a year later, but the Congress became the first of the Red Mountain mines to make regular shipments of ore. During 1882 about five tons of ore were shipped each day to Silverton, and the ore averaged about a hundred dollars a ton. By August of the next year, the Congress employed fifteen men and shipped twenty tons a day. The first settlement on Red Mountain Divide was built nearby, and appropriately was named Congress after the mine. Another settlement was built less than a hundred yards away and named Red Mountain City. The town of Congress eventually won out. The little settlement even had a post office for nine months. Both Congress and Red Mountain City suffered, however, when the new toll road to the major Red Mountain mines bypassed them. By 1885 (about the time of this photo) Congress only had a few dozen residents. Although totally overshadowed in the boom times of the Red Mountain Mining District (between 1883 to 1893), the Congress mine continued to do well. After the Silver Panic of 1893, the other Red Mountain mines began to fold, but the Congress Mine kept on shipping ore in part because, as silver prices dropped, the Congress discovered more gold in its ore. In fact, Tom Walsh of Camp Bird Mine fame owned the Congress at the time of his big discovery at the Camp Bird. Eventually the Congress produced over a million dollars of ore. The mine and one of the houses in the area are shown in the photo above. No long lines of ore wagons were waiting to carry the ore, but the one ore wagon at the mine shows that the Congress was still shipping!

RED MOUNTAIN CITY

This group of cabins was located a short distance above the Congress Mine in an area that was originally called Red Mountain City. It was at the very top of the divide in San Juan County, and Ouray County started just fifty yards to the north. The area was so rough that the original locators were not even positive as to which county they were in. The town was laid out in four feet of snow and the cabins were all crooked on their foundations (if they had any) in the spring. Red Mountain City was on the original trail over Red Mountain and was the first actual settlement up on the divide. At one time over a hundred people lived here, but then the main trail was moved about a mile to the west near where U. S. Highway 550 is located at present. This left Red Mountain City literally high and dry. Most of the merchants simply jacked up their little cabins and pulled them around to the new "hot spot," which was called Red Mountain Town. Red Mountain City then fell to a population of only twenty or thirty almost overnight. The shaft house in the foreground was probably the Salem Mine which was also connected with the Carbon Lake Mine. They were both good early day producers, but they never grew to be major Red Mountain mines.

GUSTON

These two photographs give a good depiction of the fairly large settlement that grew up around the Guston Mine between about 1890 and 1895. The Guston was one of the Red Mountain Mining District's later blooming mines, coming into its own about the time that most of the other Red Mountain mines had passed their prime. There were many little humps or hills in the area so the town of Guston wasn't laid out in the normal rectangular way. Rather a jumble of cabins and buildings were built haphazardly around the little hills on whatever level ground was available. Guston had stores, saloons and a post office; it just didn't fit the typical mold for a town. In the top photograph, taken about 1890, the little town had definitely been well established. The Guston Mine was in the upper right hand corner. Several tents had been staked near the mine's access tunnel, probably to provide temporary housing for the miners. The town itself included the area in the hollow to the left of the mine (the ornate manager's residence was in the center of the hollow) and also the land in the foreground, where one house was under construction. A large spot had been leveled and cleared for a store, which had been completed in the photograph to the right. The black building near the middle of each photograph was the Guston Mill. In the top photo, men were cutting firewood in front of the building in the foreground and to its right was a corduroy road, which was a road made through a swampy area by laying logs on the ground.

There were many new structures in the photograph below, which was taken from almost the same angle about five years later. The tents were gone in the background and to the left was a new structure. A covered ore track leads out to the left of the mill and the mine's waste dump had grown considerably. The Guston was now down almost seven hundred feet in depth. The shaft house that had been built to the right of the mill was the access point to the Robinson Mine. The Robinson and the Guston were now worked under one management. A building that housed the coal needed for the power plant had also been built behind and to the right of the mill. An office building had been built directly in front of the mill, and a boarding house adjoined it. The house under construction had been finished and a large store had been built on the spot that was being leveled for its contruction in the photo to the left. To the left and behind the store was Guston's Congregational Church. The people of Guston were very proud of their church, since it was the only one that existed up on Red Mountain Divide. A new house, of quite some size, had been built in the foreground of the photograph below, and there were several other new buildings in the scene. In the photo at the left about 200 people were living in Guston. In the photo below, the population was more like 350. By 1897, the area was almost deserted. Guston was a silver mine and as the price of silver fell drastically, so did Guston's population.

Uncapahgre Park and   San Juan Mountains - From Dallas, Colo.

Dallas, Colorado. July 2nd 1886 - Snowy Mountains of San Juan

$\mathcal{D}$ALLAS

The upper photograph shows the small and short-lived town of Dallas, which was located on the banks of the Uncompahgre River at its junction with Dallas Creek, about three miles north of present-day Ridgway. It was a logical place for a town to be built since it was at the junction of the roads to Ouray and Telluride when coming from Montrose or other points to the north. The town of Dallas was also the terminus of the Denver and Rio Grande Railroad for a short while before the railroad was built on into Ouray in December of 1887. The ranch of Dave Wood, the largest and most famous freighter in the San Juans, could be seen across the river and slightly above the town. The Crum ranch was in the center of the square fencing. Most of the town's residences were on the west (right) side of the Uncompahgre River, while most of the businesses were on the east side of the river. By 1884, the town sported a population of over one hundred. By 1887 (about the time of this photograph), Dallas' buildings included two hotels, a saloon, a newspaper, a post office, grocery, stables and a blacksmith's shop. Unfortunately, many of these buildings were destroyed in a large fire on September 10, 1888. Most of the damaged buildings were rebuilt, but another major fire struck in the winter of 1892-93. Since the nearby town of Ridgway was doing extremely well by this time, the town of Dallas was not rebuilt and it dropped into decay.

The lower scene gives us a close view of Dallas' Main Street. The photographer, as did many of his time, gave us about all the information that we need to know by writing on his negative "Dallas, Colorado. July 2nd, 1886. Snowy Mountains of San Juans." The snowy mountains did not turn out too well in the background, but we have a pretty good view of the little settlement. Dallas was the site of a lot of early day gold placer activity — even before the Ute Indians had given up this territory. Though the Indian agents ordered the prospectors who were in the little settlement (it was then called Gold City) to leave, they refused to do so until they were sure the placer mining had played out. Later Dallas, named after George M. Dallas, then Vice-President of the United States under President Polk, became an early day transfer and freighting station. At the time of this photograph the town was just beginning to blossom. The Placer Hotel was the large two-story building. The Dallas Hotel (with the balcony out front) was just down the street. Next to it was a saloon.

$\mathcal{A}$MES

The photograph above, which was taken about 1911, shows several aspects of the Telluride Power Company's plant at Ames, site of the first ever commercial use of alternating electrical current. Electricity was quickly picked up by the mines all over the San Juans as a cheap power source, and engineers from around the world came to Ames and nearby Ilium to learn more about this newfangled use for electricity. Electricity was soon used for lighting and power by residents throughout the region. George Westinghouse helped to build the first Ames' power plant. At the time of this photo, the stone building in front of the white transmission line structure had just been built. It housed the newly purchased Pelton water turbine, which operated on a water pressure of 380 pounds per square inch. One electric generator was in the stone building and two more were in the large wooden building to the right of it. The building with the flat roof contained transformers, and to the left of that was the blacksmith's shop and several dwellings. As many as twenty-five men worked and lived in Ames at a time. Two levels of the famous Ophir Loop of the Rio Grande Southern Railroad were visible above the power house. Two of the many bridges that were placed in the Ophir Loop were also visible.

TELLURIDE

This group of burros was loaded with mine car track and was ready to leave Telluride for the trip high into the mountains. The time frame was during the 1880s but it must have been the late 1880s. The Sheridan Hotel was yet to be built, so the photo was taken before 1890. The San Miguel County Courthouse steeple was visible at the left in the photograph, and it was built in 1887. The date was therefore sometime between 1887 and 1890. There were many false-fronted business buildings along Colorado Avenue. There were also many canopies along this side of Telluride's main street since it was facing south. Some of the signs on the buildings read "Clothing and Gent's Furnishings" and "Hats and Canes." The Telluride bank was just to the right of the only brick commercial building to be seen in this photograph other than the San Miguel County Courthouse. The photo was taken from the corner of Pine and Colorado.

Pack Train, Telluride, Colo. About 1889

OPHIR

A mother and her beautiful little child had climbed a short distance from the Rio Grande Southern's tracks to get above the small settlement of "New Ophir" and to have their picture taken about 1910 by an unknown photographer. The Ophir depot was partially visible in the background, hidden behind several freight cars that had been dropped off so they could be loaded with ore from the Alta tram ore house. Some idea of the steepness and ruggedness of the mountains in the vicinity of Ophir can be gained from this photograph. The Ophir Wall, which is shown in the background, is today a favorite location for technical mountain climbers. This spot is considered to be one of the steepest, tallest and most dangerous climbs in all of the San Juans. Above the wall is the Ophir Needles, also called Cathedral Spires. The railroad tracks at the extreme right give some idea of just how steeply the tracks doubled back on each other at the Ophir Loop.

$\mathcal{T}$he photo below is an enlargement (made by Ruth Gregory) of the depot portion of the original scene. The tram house from the Alta Mine was visible at the left-hand side of the station. A short spur ran off the main track to this building so that ore from the mine could be loaded into the box cars. The Alta tram ran for some two and one-half miles north to the Alta Mill and allowed for ore to be dumped directly into the box cars. The tram was operated until about 1935. This was actually Ophir's second depot as the first was destroyed by an avalanche and the new depot was then built on this site. The agent and his family lived on the second floor of the depot. The house on the right was a boarding house, connected to the level of the depot by a steep and long wooden stairway. The structures to the left of that were boarding houses. The depot was right in the middle of the famous Ophir Loop, a huge loop made by the railroad tracks, much of which was made possible by trestles that rose a hundred feet in the air. It was a well known spot for Colorado tourists and is a mecca today for narrow gauge railroad fans.

Sams

The little settlement of Sams was located about halfway between the summit of Dallas Divide and Placerville. It was established at the point that the Dave Wood Road tied in with what is now Highway 62. The Dave Wood Road was the main trail from Montrose to Telluride, while present-day Highway 62 was the route from Ridgway to Telluride. Sams was also a stop on the Rio Grande Southern (RGS) Railroad, serving the many farming and ranching families that lived on the high mesas around Sams in the first half of the twentieth century. It is hard to believe now, but many fine grains were grown on the high mesas, including barley, wheat and rye. The RGS Railroad tracks ran behind the store. The "town" of Sams consisted of the log cabin shown in the photo below, which served as a post office and store, as well as a couple of other buildings. It was quite appropriate that a farmer and his wife and a cowboy are standing in front of the store on this day. The photograph was probably made in the 1920s or 1930s by Frank or John Rice when they were on their way to their logging operation on the Uncompahgre Plateau. The Sams post office was in continuous operation from 1903 until 1950 when the RGS stopped operation. This building burned to the ground shortly thereafter. The spot was then used for a small ski area until the present day Telluride Ski Area put it out of business.

PLACERVILLE STOCKYARDS

Placerville, named after the placer mining that was prevalent in the area at the time of its founding, has really been in two locations. Placer mining is what most people know as gold panning. The little town has always been split in half by Leopard Creek, which runs in front of the cliffs that are visible in the background. This scene might be called "West Placerville." It was the location of most of the town's stockyards, which were used for sheep and cattle that were brought into Placerville from hundreds of miles around to be shipped out on the Rio Grande Southern (RGS) Railroad. The high point of the local livestock business came in 1947 when over 1,000 carloads of animals were shipped from Placerville. Ore was also brought into Placerville for shipment from as far away as Utah. The depot and most of the commercial area of the town was on the east side of Leopard Creek. Because of the cliffs, one area could not have been seen from the other. Placerville was also a natural division point for mail and freight going up-river to Telluride and points beyond, or down river to Norwood, Nucla and Naturita. This particular day was a busy one. The RGS trains (there were two of them) were just arriving and soon these men would be busy loading the cattle cars.

DURANGO, 1893

Durango was a thriving railroad, coal and smelter town about 1893 when this photograph was taken. A large part of the Denver and Rio Grande's expanding railroad yard can be seen in the middle right of the photo. Huge coal deposits in the area furnished inexpensive fuel for the smelters and for the railroad locomotives, which brought the ore to the smelters and on the return trip took supplies to the mines. In the foreground were the coke ovens which baked the soft coal into a form that produced an intense smokeless heat (much like charcoal) when it was burned in the smelting process. Across the river was a mill owned by Thomas Graden, who also owned a Durango lumber yard and store. Two different bridges crossed the Animas River at this point, one for the railroad and one for wagon traffic. The highway to Cortez still uses this crossing. The central school and La Plata County Courthouse were in the middle of the view. The red light district was on the left alongside the river. The flat top mesa in the background is the present location of Ft. Lewis College.

Durango, Colo. 1

PLACERVILLE

The glass negative of the photo above was unfortunately cracked, yet it is a good view of what might be called "East Placerville." These two freighters are evidently hauling merchandise for a store and they haven't hesitated to pile the goods up high on the wagons. Placerville was first prospected in May of 1876 by Colonel S. H. Baker, who headed a prospecting party of nine men. News of his discovery of placer gold soon spread, and a town was laid out in 1877. The original location was at this spot, but in 1879 a man named Smith located a cabin about a mile downstream. Gradually a community built up around his cabin. When the Rio Grande Southern (RGS) came to town they built their depot and facilities on the original location and the town moved back up stream. The RGS Railroad's tracks were to the right in the photograph.

GALLOWAYS, PLACERVILLE

Placerville was at the crossroads of routes from Ridgway, Telluride and Norwood. It was a remote area, and therefore a place where the horse, the automobile, the stage and the train could all be found as late as the 1940s. In this photo, taken about 1925 or 1930, a group of travelers have stopped at Galloways, which advertised that "Stage with U. S. mail leaves here for Norwood, Naturita and points west at 7 A. M." A painted hand pointed to the Placerville Hotel. Bales of barbed wire were piled out front, waiting for a rancher to pick them up. Ranchers, miners and tourists all mingled in Placerville.

ORIGINAL SAN JUAN COUNTY COURTHOUSE

This building was the original San Juan County Courthouse, built in 1874, back in the days when Howardsville was the county seat of San Juan County. The cabin was located on the south side of Cunningham Creek and was also used as an early day church and meeting hall. Later that year, Silverton began to grow in size and importance. One night, unknown men pirated the county's records to Silverton, which then became the county seat. Howardsville was in a good location for a town, at the intersection of the road that ran from Silverton to Animas Forks and the one that ran over Stony Pass to Del Norte and the San Luis Valley, which was the original route into the San Juans for most prospectors. George Howard, one of the early San Juan county pioneers, built his log cabin in the vicinity in 1871 and the settlement was later named after him. The courthouse was subsequently used as a school. (Ruth Gregory's mother attended the Howardsville school for a while.) It was abandoned at the time of this photo and was later used as a barn. In the early fifties, the historical importance of the structure was recognized, but it totally burned in a fire in August of 1954. The Silverton Northern Railroad tracks ran past the cabin to the left in this scene.

HOTEL GALENA, HOWARDSVILLE

There were no big mines at the actual site of Howardsville, but from an early date it became a major milling and shipping center. There was also no real commercial area, just a general scattering of cabins and businesses. The Hotel Galena in Howardsville was built for Ruth Gregory's grandmother, Mrs. Ellen Shaw, who owned and operated it. Grandmother Shaw was shown here standing in the doorway. Luella Shaw, Ruth's mother, was the woman at the far right in the photograph. The store next to the Hotel Galena sold general merchandise. Someone had stopped their buggy so that they could also get into the photo. Note how the grade was built up under the hotel so that it stood three or four feet higher than the street. It was necessary since the Animas River regularly flooded the entire area during heavy spring runoffs.

EUREKA

The large Sunnyside Mill dominated Eureka Mountain, which was directly behind the town of Eureka, in this photograph taken in 1917. (The big white building with the bell tower to the far left in the center was the school that Ruth Gregory attended in the first grade.) If you look carefully, several Model T's were visible in the scene. Eureka was one of the first towns established in the San Juans. The Eureka post office opened on August 9, 1875, and operated continuously until May of 1942. The town was located a few miles to the northeast of Howardsville. Eureka was at its peak during the first quarter of the twentieth century. The Sunnyside Mine was the basic reason for the town's existence. The mine was discovered in 1873 and was located quite a distance up Eureka Gulch at 12,300 feet elevation. However, it was at Eureka that the Sunnyside's mills were built, with the major part of its production taking place between 1917 and 1948, when two and a half million tons of ore were shipped out worth over fifty million dollars. This 500 ton mill was constructed in 1917. A large part of the mill's components came from the Gold Prince Mill in Animas Forks. The Sunnyside Mill was the first commercial lead-zinc flotation plant in North America. During the 1950s the mine's production gradually decreased and many of Eureka's buildings were moved to Silverton — some were even transported to the Idarado Mine at Red Mountain.

$\mathscr{L}$RONTON

The stage coach had arrived in Ironton (originally called Copper Glen) on a wonderfully sunny day in the late 1880s. Ironton was at its prime. The unknown photographer was to shoot quite a few images on this occasion, and a large number of people gathered about so as to be included in the photographs. It was mid-summer and the passengers on the stage in the lower photo were riding in an open conveyance. Only four horses were needed on this day because of the lightness of the load. At the left, a teamster or prospector also stopped to get in the photo. To the far right was another pack train which was loaded with supplies for the mines. The scene above was taken the same day and even included some of the same people. The pack string of mules had moved up the street and had been joined by a man and his bicycle. The building on the far left was a hotel. Faintly, on the mountain at the end of Main Street, could be seen the Saratoga Mill. Ironton boasted that its Main Street was a mile long, with hardly a structure that was located on a street other than Main. It was basically a supply town for the mines and settlements nearby. For a short time Ironton was the northern terminus for the Silverton Railroad. In 1890, the U.S. census officially listed its population as 323. Ironton had its own water works, electric plant, post offices, two churches (a steeple is visible over the building left of center in the photo to the left) and a fire department. Because of the fall in silver prices Ironton was going downhill fast by 1895 and by 1910 it was almost deserted.

$\mathscr{S}$NEFFELS, COLORADO

This scene showed the little settlement of Sneffels that established itself across the creek of the same name well before the Revenue Mine and Mill complex existed. Porter's original store and post office were on the right, but at the time of this photo the original roughhewn log cabins had been covered with siding to give them a more dignified look. That portion of Porter's complex shown at the extreme right was the original store and post office, but the cabin had now been converted into a residence. The two-story building was the new general store and post office and connected to the left was a pool hall and saloon. Several men were enjoying them-selves on this fine day by sitting on the porch. The separate buildings to the left of Porter's complex were all houses. In the foreground to the left are John Ashenfelter's barns. Ashenfelter was the biggest and best freighter in Ouray at the time. Besides his freight wagons and mule teams, Ashenfelter also rented horses to the five or six hundred miners who lived in the vicinity to use when they wished to visit Ouray or Telluride on their day off. At the extreme left of the photo was another house which stood until just recently. Its majestic bay window fascinated all who saw it. Stony Mountain rises in the background and is a huge, steep volcanic plug that has so little soil that virtually nothing lives on its slopes. It has also been just about as barren of valuable minerals as it has been of vegetation.

Chapter 4
Women and Children

IN STARK CONTRAST to the dirty, carefree prospectors and miners stood the women and children of the San Juans. Women and children were a lot more common than were usually portrayed — approximately one-third of all mining men had their families living with them. The women worked long and hard hours, yet they always found the time and effort to bring a sense of culture and domestication to the mountains. With the children came laughter and joy, although the death rate among the young was deplorably high. Every week's newspaper carried at least one more death notice for a young child.

A miner tried to spend every free moment that he could with his family. The women and children were usually left behind, in one of the San Juan's larger towns where the women could feel safer and the children could attend a good-sized school. There were, however, some families that accompanied their men up to the highest and most remote of locations. Strange yet comforting was the sight of geraniums sitting in a window of a rough log cabin high in the mountains. It seemed even more out of place if the window had lace curtains.

A common practice during the nineteenth century was for children to make their own fun rather than having store-bought toys. It was even more of a necessity in the remote San Juans. Most manufactured toys were just too expensive or perhaps not available at all. Assay cups were used for tea sets. Dolls were sometimes made from rags or scraps of cloth. Riding the wild burros that prospectors had abandoned in the mountains was always great fun. On occasion, a carnival or circus might come to town and the family would scrape up money for the children to attend. Skiing was popular in the winter but it was a dangerous sport because boots were strapped directly onto long planks of wood. Sleds were made from old crates and barrels. The Ouray hot springs pool was popular after it was built in the 1920s and families might travel many miles to enjoy a swim.

Chipeta and Child

Chipeta was the wife of the famous Ute chief, Ouray. (This photograph of Chipeta was taken by Ruth's Aunt Cora in Olathe, Colorado about 1910.)   At the time of this photo, Chief Ouray had been dead for some thirty years and the Utes had been banished to Utah from Colorado for almost the same amount of time. Chipeta was alone and forgotten during most of that period and became virtually blind from cataracts. However, Chipeta was rediscovered by the whites shortly after the turn of the century, and it became very popular to have her attend parades, fairs and festivals in Colorado. Chipeta was a very loving woman. Although she couldn't have any children, she adopted dozens of needy Ute infants. She was also thoughtful and made many beaded buckskin items as thank you gifts for small favors that were done for her. In return, she was highly regarded by the people of the Western Slope of Colorado.

Lady's Club at the Pool

A commonly seen photograph (and one that appears in Chapter Seven of this book) is one taken after the 1929 flood, when Ouray's men and boys rolled up their sleeves and got the swimming pool mucked out and back into operation very quickly. As usual, there was a squadron of women doing support duty on that same day. They appear here, organized and ready to serve lunch or snacks to the men. Those that have been identified included Mary Stanley Granbow and Marquerite Childress MacLennan in the top row and Mrs. Charlie Fritsch, Erma Hestwood, Blanche Downer, Ruth Rice, Louise Israel and Annie Doran in the front row.

A Victorian Home

The stiffness of the women in this Frank Rice photograph was caused by the long exposure time of early day cameras, during which the subjects had to sit perfectly still. Even so, Frank Rice's mother (the woman on the left) had a blurry image because of movement. The people of the Victorian age loved to decorate everything to excess, and the variety of objects in this room indicate that the Ouray home of Mrs. Gordon Kimball was no exception to the rule. At the upper left corner, bird's wings (probably a raven's) hung from the wall. Below that was what looked like a huge hornet's nest. Another set of smaller bird wings hung on the wall to the left of the stove, and a live bird was in the cage a little further to the left. The lady's fine crystal and silver had been set out for the photographer, as well as several items of pottery and cut glass. In contrast, a spittoon sat on the floor. A kerosene or white gas lamp hung over the dining room table, placing the time frame before the general use of electricity in the San Juans (early 1900s). The lady's dining room sported a fine stove with a long expanse of exposed stove pipe. Although this looks unattractive to us today, it had a very practical effect in allowing every little bit of heat to escape into the room before the smoke entered the chimney. As we can tell from the many plants in the windows, this lady was a gardener and brought most of her projects indoors for the winter.

An Outing in Silverton

A large group of women and men seemed to be ready for a good time on a day's outing in the San Juan Mountains. Most of the women were riding burros while the men were either riding horses or on foot. The women of the San Juans lived in a harsh and remote region, yet they were generally responsible for bringing culture to their local areas. They were usually able to do so, and yet still retain their humor and their love of life. The men also seemed able to forget their harsh life. At least one man in this photo appeared to be riding his burro backwards! It was a festive and party-like atmosphere. Today people can be seen, early on summer mornings, getting ready to go out on excursions in their jeeps or on motorcycles. They don't really look all that much different than this group.

ℒADIES' OUTING

These ladies seemed to be all dressed up and ready for an outing into the mountains around Ouray in August of 1886. In fact, they are a little too dressed up for the occasion. Although they wore the simple, black "every day" dresses of the time, several have chosen their best hats for the occasion. They were from the left: Mrs. Sparks, Mrs. Kedsie, Mrs. George Wright, Mrs. Gordan Kimball, Mrs. Alexander, Susie Nash, Mrs. Vorbeck, Mrs. Werner, Mrs. Hildenbrandt and Mrs. Miner. All of the women rode side-saddle — both a difficult and dangerous undertaking in the mountains. A woman had to be much more athletic than a man to ride in such a way. Their trusty steeds were, in this case, burros — probably the most sure-footed and dependable of all their choices. However, the burro could also be one of the most obstinate of animals, which is the reason for the large whip in the hand of the lady to the left and the sticks and ropes in the hands of most of the other ladies. The corral in the background probably held the little burros, although they were also left at times to fend for themselves on the local mountain sides. Most of these women seemed to be really having fun, even though there were a few somber faces in the group.

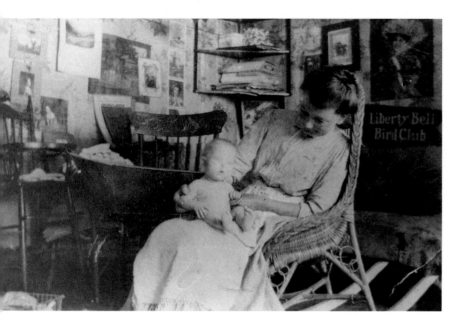

Lady with Baby

This proud mother had just given her baby a bath in the small wash tub which sat on the chair behind her. The baby's wooden high chair was to the left of the tub, and a stack of diapers waited behind the chair. Now it seemed time for her to rock the baby to sleep in the wicker rocking chair. The walls were decorated with the typical Victorian clutter of the time. One wonders what the Liberty Bell Bird Club might have been? Perhaps it was connected with the Liberty Bell Mine near Telluride.

Who is this Lady?

This lady shows up in quite a few the Gregory's photographs but no one knows who she was. (Ruth would love to know the name or history of this woman.) She is fascinating for she appears to have been very lively and agile for her age. She shows up in a variety of poses and situations throughout the Gregory photograph collection. In this scene she was riding side-saddle at a time when most women her age would have traveled in a carriage. The large rock in the background of this photograph placed the lady in front of the Kimball House on Oak Street in Ouray. The Kimball house was originally built by Charles McIntyre but was soon sold to Gordon Kimball who lived in this structure for forty-five years. It didn't always look like this. Previously it had burned to the ground and had only been recently rebuilt at the time of this photograph. Gordon Kimball bought a hardware store that had been started by Otto Mears in Ouray. As a store owner, Kimball grubstaked several Ouray prospectors and ended up with interests in many of the local mines.

*G*USTON WOMEN

These women posed on the steps of an unknown building at Guston in 1890. Even at such a high and remote mining camp, it is obvious that they were, for the most part, a well-educated, well-bred group who brought a real touch of class to this remote outpost. None of the names of the women are known. We wonder what kind of social or cultural affair brought them together on this particular day?

RIDGWAY POST OFFICE

The employees of the Ridgway Post Office proudly posed outside their building on this bright and sunny summer day on August 1, 1911. The two little boys on the right had also decided to get into the picture. The Ridgway Post Office was originally opened in the Ridgway Bank Building on October 1, 1890. At the time of this photograph, however, the post office was located in what was called the Jeffers building (Mrs. Jeffers of Ouray was the owner) on the south side of Clinton Street near Cora Street. The post office moved to this location in 1906 and remained there until 1916. The post office was then returned to the Ridgway Bank Building from 1916 until the 1930s, when it again returned to this location in the Jeffers Building. We think of women in the work place as a relatively new phenomenon but lots of women held jobs in the past. Their opportunities were usually limited and their pay was much less than their male counterparts. The post office was an exception, however, as there were many early-day women postmasters. At the time of this photograph Mrs. Willa Johnson held the position. Presumably she was the woman to the right and her employees were to the left in this photograph.

𝒯HE PARK HOTEL

Ridgway's Park Hotel was so named because it faced the town's large park that still exists between what was the original railroad depot and Ridgway's business district which began on Lena Street. The visitors to the Park Hotel would have looked directly out over the park with a full view of the depot and the beautiful Courthouse Range. Some of the guests evidently used the chair located on the second floor balcony to get a better view. The Park Hotel also made it a point to hire good-looking waitresses, which helped to pull men into the establishment. It was expected that most single waitresses were looking for an acceptable husband. On this particular day, the employees of the hotel were posing in their best attire on the plank sidewalk. Evidently the employees had been joined by a few of the hotel's "regular customers" who stand to the left. The man with the apron near the center of the scene was evidently the cook or a cook's helper. The Park Hotel was used as the Ridgway school for awhile in the 1930s, when the town's regular schoolhouse burned down.

Sisters of Mercy

Not all of the women in the San Juans were looking to get married. The St. Joseph Miners Hospital was opened in Ouray in 1887 by the Order of Sisters of Mercy. One of the sisters stands behind the automobile in this scene. The hospital was a substantial structure built of native stone and brick. The sisters put out a call for funds in 1886 and raised the necessary money within months. Many of Ouray's citizens contributed to the project, but most of the funds came from the nearby big mines. The sisters became a very important part of the Ouray community. There was no insurance for miners in those days. However, a one dollar per month subscription to the hospital would get you treatment for any illness or accident. When times got tough for the hospital in the late 1890s, Tom Walsh paid off the sisters' mortgage. In 1905 the addition, seen here to the left and back, was added. Shortly after this photo was taken in 1920, the hospital was sold to Dr. Carl Bates, and he operated it for many years as the Bates Hospital in connection with his hot cave baths at the present-day Weisbaden. Later the hospital was run by Dr. Edward Spangler and owned by the Idarado Mine. In 1952, when federal authorities said the hospital must meet new codes or shut down, the latter was chosen. The building was reopened as the Ouray County Historical Museum in 1971 and now houses a very fine collection of photographs and artifacts.

A SICK HOUSE, OURAY

At the turn of the century, the owners of the house on the right advertised that it was a home for the sick. "Lodging 25 and 35" probably indicated the monthly rates that were charged. The location was Ninth Avenue on the west side of Main Street in Ouray. The lodging was probably for injured or sick miners. Mining was a hazardous profession. Men could be injured by dynamite that exploded prematurely, from huge slabs of rock that fell unexpectedly or by heavy machinery that didn't operate as expected. They could fall down a shaft, be caught in an avalanche or have a shaft cable snap. Or it could be a more "common" cause of injury or illness like a hernia that didn't heal, pneumonia or typhoid. There was no health insurance for miners in those days. If they were lucky and they had some money saved, they could come to recuperate for a month or two in an establishment like this while they healed. Usually it was unmarried, older women who would care for them. In this scene children played on the front porch to the left. It appeared that two houses were built together; the one on the left (in the middle) may have been the residence of the man, young woman, dog and probably the children. The house on the right was the sick house, probably run by the two women in the front.

Women Underground

This photograph is highly unusual and very likely to have been staged because many miners considered it to be extremely unlucky for women to be underground. Obviously these two women were not workers and were not dressed for any type of real underground work. The woman at the right was "double jacking" — a procedure by which one man held the drill and another used the sledge hammer. The woman on the left was breaking off loose rock. Although not all miners considered it unlucky for women to be underground, it was simply unheard of for the women to actually work underground before the 1970s. These men did not seem to mind, however. The lighting for the work in this scene was supplied by candles, thereby dating the photo to before 1910 when carbide lights came into common use. Miners were usually issued three or four candles for their ten- to twelve-hour shift. It was placed in his hat like the women have done or placed in a metal candle holder which was stuck into cracks in the rocks or nearby timbers.

JOHN RICE FAMILY

The family of John Rice had chosen the front steps of their Oak Street home in Ouray to have their photograph taken in 1885. John came to Ouray in 1883 with his wife Grace and their children Elizabeth, also known as Bessie (the little girl to the left) and Frank (the boy at the center), as well as a baby who evidently died soon after this photo was taken. Grace Rice was to the right and her sister on the left. The woman in the center is unknown. John Rice worked in the post office, eventually becoming the Ouray postmaster. He was later forced to leave his office because of politics and afterwards became a bookkeeper. In 1910 he opened the Rice Lumber Company, which still exists in approximately the original location, across the Uncompahgre River from Rice's Oak Street home. Another unfortunate tragedy struck the Rice family when Elizabeth died of scarlet fever in 1899 at the young age of fifteen. Several of the family's pets shared this scene as well as a Navajo rug that the Rices were evidently proud of. Little Frank Rice grew up to take many of the photographs that are now a part of the Ruth and Marvin Gregory Collection. He had a great love for Ouray's history and wrote *Historical Notes: Ouray County and Its Mines*. Rice never lived to see his book published, but it has been a primary source for students of Ouray history.

TEMPLE OF MUSIC

Not all of the women in the San Juans lived what was termed "a respectable life." On this day some of the women at the Temple of Music posed for the photographer. It was quite unusual to get an interior shot of a bordello. Presumably, the musical part of the name for the establishment came from the old wind-up phonograph. Music, however, was probably one of the last things that Ouray's men had on their minds when they visited these women. Ouray's Red Light District was on both sides of Second Street between Seventh and Eighth Avenues. Other such establishments included The Bon Ton, The Bird Cage, The Monte Carlo, The Morning Star, The Gold Belt and The Club. Although houses of prostitution were technically illegal from the time the city of Ouray's first laws were passed, they were tolerated and, in fact, often licensed. The women who worked here were required to get periodic medical checkups to show that they were physically sound. At one time there were almost fifty women working in Ouray in houses of ill repute. The large Ashenfelter horse barns were around the corner and in the next block, so the ladies of the night probably used plenty of perfume. When the barns burned, the fire took the Temple of Music and the Bon Ton (no relation to the restaurant) with it. By that time Ouray's citizens were trying to make the town more respectable, so neither establishment was rebuilt.

Women on Horseback

The two women in the photo below were very avant-garde for the time since they were not riding their mounts side-saddle. Probably they or their family had ranches in the area and they were actual "working" cowgirls. On this day they had ventured forth to Placerville, one of the greatest sheep and cattle shipping points in western Colorado during the first half of the twentieth century. Some ranchers brought their herds to Placerville from as far as Utah to ship them to market aboard the Rio Grande Southern Railroad. The Placerville blacksmith shop was on the right.

Children on Oak Street

The play toys of this group of children included several burros! It was quite typical at a time when many of the hard working animals were simply let go to roam after they could no longer do hard service as a transporter. A small corral was evidently built to the left of the cabin to help keep the burros contained. Children's toys in the San Juans often consisted of common household items. These boys and girls seemed quite comfortable with their burros. The children's mothers looked on from the front porch of the family's log home in the background. They were probably quite anxious about the baby in the carriage in the foreground. This cabin is now gone, but the large rock to the left of the house is certainly the same as ever. These children were probably from the Charles and Gertrude Cornforth family. Their cabin was built sometime around 1890. Cornforth was a partner with A. U. Smith in a transfer and express company which was located in a building that still stands at the southeast corner of Seventh Avenue and Oak Street in Ouray. The transfer company took supplies off the train and transported them wherever they needed to go. Note just how narrow Oak Street (which runs to the right of the cabins) was in those days. There was no such thing as a front yard for these cabins.

A WOMAN IN HIGH PLACES

Women followed their men to some pretty remote places in the San Juans, but surely none were in a more hazardous location than that of the lady standing in front of the door to the tent in this photograph. She was at one of the mines on Gold Hill, which was directly to the north of Ouray but was at least 1,000 feet higher in elevation. She could be a cook who was living at this spot or merely a visitor for the day. Regardless of her status she made quite an effort to get here. (Ruth made this photo from a stereo card in her possession which identifies this scene as part of the American Nettie Mine but, if that is the case, it must have been very early in its operation.)

GEORGE WASHINGTON'S BIRTHDAY

Some of Ouray's children were evidently celebrating George Washington's birthday by dressing up as George and Martha Washington on this special winter day about the turn of the century. The teachers and parents obviously thought it was a very cute scene and called in the local photographer to capture the scene for posterity. The children stood in front of Ouray's brick school building. In the background was Judge William Story's fine house, later used as a boarding house and then a mortuary. It is now owned and lovingly cared for by Bob and Pam Larson. Only a few of the children in this photo have been identified. The girl who is second from the left was Dorothy Davidson. The boy and girl who are third and fourth from the right have been identified as being from the Rucker family. Some of these children seemed to be really enjoying themselves, while others seemed to be quite peeved to have to dress up in costumes and hold hands with members of the opposite sex.

INTERIOR OF SCHOOL

This interior shot of a one-room schoolhouse was made in the San Juans about the turn of the century. The teacher had her class well under control with everyone sitting very properly at their desks with their hands folded in front of them. All of the children seemed fairly young, probably being in the first to third grades. Teaching aids had been pinned on the walls of the classroom — rabbits, grapes and the alphabet. The teacher was instructing during a time when an unmarried, educated woman often ended up with this job. In the San Juans, women didn't usually keep an unmarried status for long because of the abundance of unattached men in the area and the shortage of available women.

$\mathcal{M}$INNIE HOLADAY

Minnie Holaday was a local girl who attended school at Portland and then at Dallas, both now ghost towns. She took her teacher's exam and began teaching at the age of seventeen at the Ouray County school at Alkali Creek. To help ends meet she also worked as the janitor of the school. When she saved enough money, she attended the State Normal School (now the University of Northern Colorado) at Greeley. She worked for a doctor as a nanny to pay for her education. After graduation she came back to Ouray with her degree and became Ouray County Superintendent of Schools from 1898 to 1902. She quit to marry William Rathmell, one-time Ouray County judge and owner of the local abstract company. They had a son in 1905. After he was grown, Minnie again served as Superintendent of Schools for Ouray County from 1922 to 1924. She also taught at the Ouray school from 1926 to 1933. In 1933 she went to work with her husband at their Ouray abstract company and then ran the business by herself after his death in 1943. She died in 1954. Minnie Holaday was an example of a true pioneer woman.

MRS. RICE AT BEAR CREEK FALLS

Mrs. Frank Rice had accompanied her friend Dorothy Davidson (who took the photo) up onto the Million Dollar Highway in 1917, but this time she seemed to have chosen a little burro for her transportation instead of Frank's car. Evidently the women were off to explore some trail that the car couldn't conquer. A drinking cup hangs off her saddle horn. A large bank of dirt ran along the edge of the highway as a safety measure. The stone safety walls hadn't been installed alongside the road yet. Today there is no "lip" along the edge of the highway because the snow plows need to push the snow off the highway in the winter. Bear Creek Falls is under the bridge in the background. It comes through an outcrop of shale, much of which can be seen lining the road.

ℰARLY DAY "CAR SEAT"

This early-day baby carrier was constructed by Ruth Gregory's Uncle Ernest Shaw who used it to transport his son, George, through the deep mountain snows. It was unique enough that someone had to get a picture of it. The family dog, Scroggins, was at the left. Children had to learn to adapt to the harsh conditions of the San Juans. Ruth vividly remembers being transported as a small child of five under conditions similar to this scene. Her mother was working as a cook at the Green Mountain Mill, which was located about five miles above Silverton in Cunningham Gulch. The people at the mine depended on pack trains to bring them supplies. One winter, when the roads became so bad that supplies couldn't be brought in, Ruth's mother hitched a team to a sled and headed with Ruth for Howardsville. It was only two or three miles away but it was a dangerous and frightening ride. Ruth's mother was constantly worried that the sled would tip over but they got the supplies and returned to the mine. Ruth got so cold during the trip that she awoke the next day with the croup. The men at the mine took turns holding her. The only medicine available was an occasional spoonful of whiskey mixed with sugar. It was finally decided that Ruth and her mother needed to get to Silverton to the doctor. It took hours to get to Howardsville (even though it was less than two miles) since the horses were constantly lunging through the deep snows. There they caught the train to Silverton. It was the last train to go out for some time because of the heavy snows. With proper medicine and care, Ruth soon recovered.

CHILD ON BURRO

This child's parents had saddled up their burro and placed their little son or daughter in the saddle for a portrait. The location and the child's identity are both unknown but it surely makes a cute scene.

EARLY DAY SCHOOL BUS

About the turn of the century a wagon or an open carriage was often used as a school bus. The driver of this team was Muriel Cornforth Evans. The identity of the other woman is unknown. The location was in the vicinity of today's sewer plant to the north of Ouray. The children had probably walked down from the Gold Hill or Bachelor mines. We tend to remember the hard work done by the brave men who first came to the San Juans. What we sometimes forget is that women were usually right behind them, and that they, too, did hard and dangerous work. They also tended to have a much needed, civilizing nature. The two women were gathering up children who needed schooling and, although the road was covered with ruts and mud, they were having absolutely no trouble handling the two-horse team. It took real nerve to be able to handle this job — perhaps a task that no man could handle!

ℳARIE OLSON

Children have always been a priceless treasure to their parents and Marie Olson's parents spared no expense to have their child's photograph taken at Michael Brumfield's photography studio in Ouray. The ornate carriage and umbrella were probably props used in the shop, although they could have been owned by the Olson family. Nothing else is known about Marie Olson's life but she was obviously a well-loved and very cute baby.

$\mathcal{M}$INIATURE STAGE

For many years Louis King operated his carriage-making shop right next door to the Ouray City Hall, which was shown in the background of this photograph. King, an early arrival in Ouray, opened a blacksmith shop, livery and carriage-making establishment on the corner of Main Street and Seventh Avenue in 1877 and continued his occupation at that location until his building burned down in the late 1880s. Then he moved to this location where he practiced his trade until he closed down his business and retired. This miniature, one-half scale Overland Stage was one of his masterpieces. It was authentic in every detail and was an immediate and great hit with Ouray's children. At least fourteen children (if you include the older boy who was acting as driver) had piled into or on top of the convey-ance for this photograph. The two full-sized horses totally overpowered the small stage. The small overland coach was so unique that it was taken to parades and fairs all over Colorado and has shown up in photographs as far away as Salt Lake City. King was certainly one man who knew his trade well, and the children loved him.

$\mathcal{U}$te Indians

These Utes had their photograph taken by George Moore in Montrose, Colorado. The San Juans were part of the ancestral home for the Ute Indians. Nevertheless, when the white man came to Colorado, their rights were virtually ignored. The Utes were given no choice but to move. They were often lied to and cheated by the white man. Yet during all of this, the Utes remained basically peace-loving and friendly. After they were moved into Utah in August of 1881, the Tabeguache Utes would often come back through Montrose and Ouray. They had retained hunting rights in the San Juans, and many of their extended families were split between the Southern Ute reservation near Durango, Colorado and the Uintah and Ouray reservations in northwestern Utah. As they traveled back and forth, they were often seen camping in fields and would sometimes ask for food from the local families. The Utes and the whites got along fairly well, and the Utes were often invited to participate in fairs and parades. The Ute women used cradle boards for their young children. It was an easy way for the Ute mothers to keep their children under control while they worked. The children also felt very protected and content in the cradle boards. The Utes were famous for their soft and supple buckskin clothing and purses and for their beautiful beading. If you look closely, several examples can be seen in this photo, yet the man at the left rear wore what looked like a cavalry uniform. Many of the Utes had acted as scouts for the United States army in the mid-nineteenth century — especially in forays against their traditional enemies.

DENVER POST NEWSPAPER BOYS

Around the turn of the century the *Denver Post* kept a huge crew of newspaper boys busy selling and delivering papers in Ouray. It was a time when finances were tight and many of these boys might have had no other source of spending money. Seventeen paper boys were visible in this Erickson photograph, and they all carried the New Year edition of the paper. The larger boy in the middle seemed to be taking good care of his little brother, the smallest boy in the group. They all wore ties and hats and five of the boys evidently used burros for the delivery of their papers. The location of this photograph was at Sixth Avenue, just below Main Street. The trail to the amphitheater was highly visible on the hillside behind the boys. It led to several mines which were operating in that area including the Portland, Cascade and Woodstock. Ouray's City Hall was visible on the far left of the scene as well as many of Ouray's new brick business buildings.

Camp Bird School

The school at the Camp Bird Mine was a simple one-room affair, yet it was very nicely done. Although there were some 500 men working at or near the Camp Bird, not very many of them brought their families to live with them — even though approximately half were married. The reason was the harshness of the high altitude. Even Ouray was considered to be too high in elevation by some of the families. The dangers of pneumonia and other respiratory diseases were very real, yet the children in this photo seem to be a hardy lot. The teacher was at the right with two of her older girl pupils — probably important helpers in teaching the younger children. Two big boys were in front of the school's small porch and entry. By this age, boys were usually working at menial tasks in the mine. It would, therefore, be suspected that the families of these boys had high hopes for them and were expecting them to continue on to college. The porch helped to keep out the cold winter winds. It must have been summer, however, or nearly so, as there was no snow on the ground and most of the children wore no coats. The wooden planks that the children were sitting on were probably rejects and scraps from the mine. They may have been brought over for use as kindling in the school's large pot-bellied stove. The children at the far left sat on a covered box which probably contained the coal for the stove. Everyone seemed to be very dignified and appropriately serious in the photo. They were definitely much more formal in their matters of schooling in those days.

OURAY DANCE

The Ouray High School of 1918 evidently had a dance which was called the "Sod Buster Reunion." Ouray was a mining town and was relatively affluent and sophisticated. Ouray's population generally looked down on ranchers and farmers with a considerable amount of disdain. The students showed up for the dance, for the most part, in overalls and other unkempt or dowdy clothes. Several of the boys couldn't bring themselves to dress down and they appear in suits and ties — quite snappy for the time. This attitude caused considerable friction between Ridgway (basically a ranching and farming community) and Ouray (primarily a mining town). (Ruth obtained this photo from Norma Schwend who was one of the girls in the photo.)

$\mathcal{H}$OWARDSVILLE SCHOOL

This looks like Parent's Day at the Howardsville school at either the beginning or end of the school year. It was evidently an extremely windy day as everyone's hair was blowing and several of those present are tightly holding on to their hats. The Howardsville school was a one-room schoolhouse. There were twelve children present on this day, along with several older boys and girls who may or may not have been students. (Ruth Gregory attended the first grade in Howardsville.)

$\mathcal{I}$RONTON SCHOOL

This photograph is identified as being either the Ironton or Guston school around the turn of the century. There were no older boys in the scene, since they were probably already at work in the mines. The population of Ironton and Guston were declining rapidly and the school looked pretty tired and worn. Most children stayed in the bigger San Juan towns while their fathers worked at the mines in the nearby mountains; but a few (as shown by the photograph at left) followed their parents right up into the high country. It was a dangerous but exciting life.

$\mathcal{L}$OG HILL SCHOOL

The school house located at Log Hill stood in sharp contrast to the neat and tidy school at the Camp Bird Mine or the large, brick school building in Ouray. It was a small and rough-hewn log cabin that seems to be in the last stages of construction in this scene. Rocks still hold down the tar paper on the top of the front porch. Most of the boys and girls were children of nearby farmers and ranchers. They may not have had as rich a benefactor as Thomas Walsh and there may not have been as many of them as at the Ouray school, but they and their young teacher seemed to have been just as proud and well-mannered as their counterparts.

Ouray School Children

Just a portion of Ouray's grade school children posed before the new brick elementary school house in the 1890s. There were many more children attending the school at that time than at present, since Ouray's population hovered around 2,000 and families were much larger then. There were probably only two grades presented in this photograph, as verified by the fact that only two teachers were present. Both teachers looked like they were harsh and stern disciplinarians — a necessary trait with that many pupils. There were thirty to forty children in each grade at the time. A large variety of bright and shining faces are presented in this scene. Dress included everything from cowboy outfits to sailor suits for the boys and fancy dresses to simple outfits for the girls. The little girl near the middle at the very corner of the stone walls carried an umbrella as did the boy in the row just above her. Back at the time of this photograph, many of these wonderful children didn't live to see adulthood because of the dreaded diseases that often took their lives. Yet every one of the children obviously had a personality that can still be determined, at least in part, by simply carefully looking at each little face. This wall still stands, but the school is long gone. The cornerstone of the old school has been inserted into the southwest corner of the wall around the present school playground as a vivid reminder of what was once the pride of all Ouray.

GIRL WITH DOLLS

The unknown little girl at the left had done a wonderful job of arranging her child-sized table for tea, and two of her special dolls had been invited to join the party. She had quite properly put on her apron and was certainly proud of the toys that are shown with her.

RUTH ON RUNNING BOARD

The little girl on the running board of this car was Ruth Gregory. Nowland Mesa was a fruit-growing area near Hotchkiss, and on this particular day Ruth and her family were taking part in an annual harvest festival and parade. Pumpkins, squash, wheat and corn made up just a few of the decorations which had been placed on the car for the parade.

GOING CAMPING

Lon Arington had his two children packed and ready to go camping in these early day "car seats." The two little girls seemed to be having a great time, while their mother didn't seem so sure about the whole matter. Lon was a freighter and most certainly would have secured the wooden boxes tightly onto the little burros since they were carrying his most precious cargo. The trip probably turned out just fine.

Chapter 5
The Snow

IN THE WINTER, THE SAN JUANS are not only some of the most beautiful but also some of the most deadly mountains in the United States. Cold is not the major problem. In fact, it is the general warmness of the area that contributes greatly to the danger. Because of the steep mountain slopes and the large amounts of wet, heavy snow, the San Juans are among the most avalanche-prone mountains in the world. The men who mined in the San Juan Mountains worked at their jobs year-round and, therefore, faced the dangerous snowslides. Several men even met their deaths in snowslides while sleeping in their own beds or eating meals in the boarding house. Men were hit by avalanches traveling on foot and on horseback. Sometimes entire towns were destroyed by snowslides.

As if the avalanches were not bad enough, the miners experienced a lot of problems with the snow itself, simply because there was so much of it. Cabins were sometimes buried to their roofs. Often all work came to a standstill because of a four- or five-foot snowfall. A heavy storm could cut visibility to a few feet and bury a miner alive — in or out of his cabin. The dangerous winter travel often isolated the miner. Some spent all winter in their cabins, high in the mountains, never going to town. They would simply work seven days a week for months at a time. In the spring, travel was not much better. The melting snow caused huge mud slides and floods, making travel difficult, if not totally impossible at times. At least with snow a man could travel by snowshoe or skis, or perhaps even on foot at night or in the early morning when the snow's crust was still frozen hard. Today conditions often are not much better. It seems humans will never harness the power of Mother Nature in the San Juans. It is a place where man must live in harmony with the seasons.

$\mathcal{B}$RINGING DOWN SLIDE VICTIMS

These men were transporting slide victims from the Virginius Mine. It had been thought that the Virginius was completely safe from snowslides, since it was located so high (12,300 feet) in the mountains and there wasn't much terrain above it to catch the snow. However, a big storm hit the area in December of 1883 and it snowed constantly for three days and nights. Slides started running all around the mine, eventually hitting the mine's boarding house. Twelve men were in the building — one in the office, four in the sitting room, two in the kitchen and five sleeping in their bunks. Four of the men were killed. Two men were buried for over twenty-four hours before they finally dug themselves out. The next day, when a rescue party was bringing the bodies down from the mine, another avalanche hit the group of thirty-two men, sweeping thirty of them down the canyon. A few men were swept just a hundred feet, others as far as a thousand feet, which included a drop over a seventy-foot cliff! At first all was still but then the men slowly started pulling themselves out of the snow. All of the men were unhurt, even the four men who had gone over the cliff. Understandably, the search for the sleds with the bodies did not resume until the weather was better and conditions not so dangerous. The bodies were then brought down to Porter's Store in Sneffels, Colorado. These images were probably taken by Porter himself since he was an accomplished photographer. It was weeks after the incident before the bodies made it to Ouray. Since all of these men weren't needed to pull the sleds, it appeared that they were more of an honor guard than a transportation team. The short man in both photos was doing double-duty as he carried a mail pouch with him.

$\mathcal{W}$INTER WAGON

During the early part of the winter the freighters could take the wheels off their wagons and replace them with runners. This worked fine as long as the snow wasn't too deep and the wagon road was well packed down. Heavier loads could actually be pulled at this time and the ride in the wagon would be a lot smoother. However, in the San Juans, winter and spring come to different elevations at different times. The flowers might be blooming in Ouray while nature is still deep in winter's slumber at a spot only one thousand feet higher in elevation. It, therefore, often became extremely difficult to take supplies from the lower valleys up to the mines in the high mountains unless the freight was loaded into wagons with wheels and then transferred into sleds. When the snow really got deep, the wagons were abandoned altogether in favor of mule or burro trains.

SNOW TUNNEL

It is unknown whether these men helped to dig this snow tunnel, but it was obviously much too big for these two men to dig alone and there was no snow or debris on the ground in this scene. It was also doubtful that the two women would have waited during the time that it would have taken for the work to be done. The trail was basically dry and the ruts in the road had probably been there for weeks. The party could be at the Riverside Slide, but more likely they were at the Waterhole Slide on the Camp Bird Road. The older man was probably a miner (perhaps at the Camp Bird) or he may have been a prospector. The men's horses were waiting behind the women.

ℋINTER PACK TRAIN

Even with sled runners, there eventually came a time when the wagons couldn't get through really deep snow. At that time the pack trains took over. The subject of these photos was the Fellin pack train which operated during the 1930s. They were on the Camp Bird Road, probably bringing supplies to the Upper Camp Bird Mine in Imogene Basin. Both of these photos show just how real the avalanche danger was along the road because of the deep snow and steep terrain, especially in the months of January, February and March. The trail was soon packed-down hard from continual use. The photograph above shows what happened if a mule stepped off the packed-down trail. The animal might sink so deep into the snow that it would have had to be dug out with snow shovels. Sometimes even that wouldn't work and the animal would be shot rather than leaving it to starve to death. The snow sometimes built up to a point where it wasn't worth the effort to continue fighting it and all travel would shut down until late springtime.

RIVERSIDE SNOW TUNNEL

The infamous Riverside Slide, which is located about four-and-a-half miles south of Ouray, has become so notorious that it has even been the topic of a recent popular song by C. W. McCall, the country western singer. The slide sometimes built up to a sixty- or seventy-foot depth over the road for a length of almost 500 feet. Until the snow became too soft in the spring, the winter "stagecoaches" (which were actually more like sleighs) went over the top of the slide since the snow was as hard as concrete. When horses or burros began breaking through the snow in the spring, a tunnel was usually dug for the stagecoach. Before the advent of motorized vehicles, a tunnel was easier to dig than a trench, and the tunnels were also a tourist attraction, which fascinated Ouray's summer visitors. Sections of the tunnel's roof would gradually fall in during the summer. This caused delays until the mess was cleared out of the way. The Ouray newspapers would usually give reports of the tunnel's shrinking length until the last sections fell sometime in late July or early August. In the early 1920s the road was moved up the mountain and tunnels were no longer necessary. In this photo, taken in the early summer of 1894, it looked like the workers had just finished constructing a tunnel.

RIVERSIDE SLIDE

Frank Rice had again gone up on the Million Dollar Highway with his family and automobile in the late 1920s. This time the canvas roof on the auto was up, probably because of a typical summer shower. There was still plenty of snow from the Riverside Slide down in the gorge, even though it was the middle of the summer. This angle, looking to the south, made it very clear why the highway was moved up the mountainside at the Riverside Slide. The original Million Dollar Highway can easily be made out below the present grade. As can be seen, it ran right into the base of the Riverside Slide, making it necessary to make long snow tunnels or cuts during most of the summer. The snow tunnel was a great tourist attraction, but it was time-consuming, costly and extremely dangerous to maintain. The road was moved up the hillside to bring it out of the worst part of the slide. Today the State of Colorado has built a huge concrete tunnel at this point. Everyone felt it would eliminate the avalanche danger but, just a few years after its construction, another victim was claimed. No matter what we do, no matter how hard we try, we seem to fail to harness nature in the rugged San Juan Mountains.

WATERHOLE SLIDE TUNNEL

The Waterhole Slide is located on the Camp Bird Road. Virtually every winter it runs hard, fast and often. It is one of the most dangerous snowslides in the San Juans. It gets its name from the "water hole" that was alongside the road, a place where men and animals could stop along the steep road to the Camp Bird Mine and take a well-deserved drink of water from a small stream that cascades down the mountainside. In January of 1909 this vicious slide caught twelve men, killing four of them as well as twenty-six head of John Ashenfelter's mules and horses. The men killed included two teamsters, one of Ashenfelter's veterinarians, and the night baker at the Camp Bird Mine who was traveling with the group. Those who were trapped told horrible tales of being totally unable to move for hours. On the other hand, the avalanche picked up a 1600-pound horse, carried it 150 feet above the road to the other side of the canyon and left it without a single scratch. The type of snow tunnel shown here was built as a defense against the slide, in the hope that the slide would run over the top of the tunnel and protect any travelers. This photo by Johnston was probably taken early in the winter or very late in spring as the Waterhole can build thirty- to fifty-feet deep.

*W*ATERHOLE SLIDE CUT

The Waterhole Slide had built to a depth of thirty or forty feet during this particular winter in the 1920s, but it was no big deal. The slide built up this deep every winter — sometimes accumulating to even fifty or sixty feet. It is obviously a huge slide. If you look closely you can make out two other vehicles several hundred feet back in the cut. The snow was still just as deep at that point. Note all the debris, packed like concrete, which was left in the side of the cut. The Waterhole runs fast and furious.

*M*INERS IN SNOW

This small group of Red Mountain miners came out of the mine to allow the photographer to take their photograph in the 1890s. The snow usually slowed outside mining activity considerably. Besides the avalanches and the difficulty of travel, the miners spent much time shoveling snow or looking for tools and materials that had been buried. Eventually the snow would get so deep that the ore could not be shipped out and the mine would be forced to shut down for lack of space to store the ore. Inside the mine the snow presented no problem as the miner worked in a year-round temperature of about fifty-six degrees.

CAMP BIRD SNOWSLIDE

The Camp Bird Mill was a real mess after the snowslide of March 17, 1906. The slide started well up on U.S. Mountain, about three quarters of a mile above the mill. It came down U. S., took a left turn, then joined with a slide coming off Hayden Mountain at the same time. The slide hit the mill and one of the Camp Bird's boarding houses. All but the engine room of the stamp mill were instantly destroyed. Luckily, there were only three men in the mill at the time of the slide. The electric lines to the Camp Bird had been cut by another earlier snow slide, the mill's machinery couldn't be operated and most of the workers were released for the day. Unfortunately one of the three men in the mill was killed. Normally there would have been fifty men at work. Tom Walsh's dog, Prince, was also found in the hard packed snow after rescuers heard heavy breathing, thought they had found one of the missing men and dug to investigate. Two days later the mill somehow caught fire and what little had remained after the avalanche was totally destroyed. Walsh quickly built a newer and bigger mill on the same site. The cyanide mill, which can be seen behind the ruins of the stamp mill, was saved.

SAGUACHE SNOWSLIDE

It is extremely difficult to get a decent photograph in the snow when there is both bright sunlight and shade involved. This deep cut through the Saguache Snowslide, which crossed the Denver and Rio Grande (D&RG) Railroad's route from Durango to Silverton, was no exception. The photographers, however, have done a good job of recording the scene. From the very first year that the Durango-Silverton branch was constructed, an attempt was made to keep the tracks open; but virtually every year the route was closed by snow for at least a short while, and sometimes for months and months. The Saguache Slide was one of the worst. On this occasion Brumfield and Gilbert, Ouray photographers, caught on film a slide that had filled the Animas Canyon to a depth of over sixty feet and for a distance of several hundred feet or more. The center of the slide was a snow tunnel and a trench such as this was made on each side. A part of the shoveling crew, which often totaled several hundred men, had climbed aboard the little narrow gauge caboose for the ride back to town. Six men rode on the back platform and one rode on the top. Just how compacted and hard the snow had become in the slide can be seen from the two trees that are vertical and horizontal in the left side of the slide. The trees had been over fifty percent exposed, yet they hung in the side of the cut as if they were glued to the snow. The avalanches ran often and deep along the D&RG's route into Silverton.

The scene to the immediate left included a photographer (either Brumfield or Gilbert). His camera case sits to the left. A snow tunnel had to be cut to a tremendous height to allow a locomotive to pass through. This gives some idea of just how deep the avalanches piled up. The snow in the tunnel had been blackened by the smoke from the locomotives. A tunnel did have an advantage over a trench in that it provided future protection from avalanches. Avalanches were such a problem that the D&RG usually had to shut down the route to Silverton every winter, during which time the people of Silverton sometimes suffered true hardships. It was then necessary to revert to the old methods used before the arrival of the railroad and send pack trains of mules to Ouray or Durango for much-needed supplies.

GREEN MOUNTAIN MILL

This photograph was taken to record what was left of the Green Mountain Mill after it was hit by a major avalanche on March 17, 1906, the same day as the Camp Bird avalanche. The owners of the Green Mountain Mill thought it to be in an area that was totally safe from snowslides, but long-time residents knew it had been built in a dangerous place. The mill had been completed just a few weeks before at a cost of $200,000. Three hours before the avalanche, the mill had shut down and all but two of the mill workers had gone to Howardsville (about two miles away) to take some time off. The avalanche tore the siding and roof from that portion of the mill that faced the avalanche path. Damage was estimated at $50,000. One of the mill workers was killed. The fact that most of the huge framing timbers were left is a testament to just how stout they were. (Ruth's mother later worked for some time as a cook at the Green Mountain Mill.) The building in the left foreground was the assay office, and the assayer was working there when the slide hit. Luckily, he was found alive several hours afterwards. The assay kiln could be seen at the far left and a woodstove stood next to the men on the left. Just about everything else had been totally destroyed.

Another Camp Bird Snowslide

Debris from a devastating snowslide had filled the kitchen of the Camp Bird Mine's boarding house at what was called Three Level in Imogene Basin on February 24, 1936. If you look very carefully in the photo above you might pick out the face of a person the photographer posed under the table, at the exact spot where rescuers found Pearl Huffman, the cook's helper and waitress, totally unhurt. Three slides (the Second Level, the Chicago and the Hidden Treasure) had all run at the same time, traveling further than they ever had before. Two men and one woman were killed at the mine that day. Rose Israel, the cook at the mine, was found dead under fifteen feet of snow, in a small shed attached to the bunkhouse. In the photo below, a man examines the wreckage in the area where Ralph Klinger, the mine's blacksmith, and Chapp E. Woods, mill superintendent, were also killed. The mine's mill, shops and a snowshed from the tunnel to the mill were all a total wreck. The mule barn was heavily damaged but none of the mules were injured. Ten men who worked on the night shift were uninjured as they slept on the second floor of the bunkhouse. Twenty-seven men were trapped underground in the mine for hours but were eventually dug out. Most people don't realize that, in an avalanche, the soft snow turns as hard as concrete. But, more than anything, it defies nature — some people are crushed while, inches away, glass is not even broken.

 NOW!

Now this is what even the native San Juaner calls deep snow! The location was probably the Virginius Mine and this was all that showed of one of its boarding houses. Just a chimney and ventilation shaft stuck out of the deep drifts. In the areas of really deep snow the miners often left their cabins like this — just making sure that they had ventilation for the fireplace, enough oxygen for breathing and that the chimney cleared the snow enough for the smoke leaving the building. The snow was actually good insulation. An added benefit was there was no need for curtains! However, they still needed to get in and out of the cabin. Since there were no tracks or signs of shoveling, it was likely that this particular cabin was not being used.

ℐNOW TRAIN

Rio Grande Southern (RGS) locomotives were usually lashed together like this when they were shoving against the RGS rotary snow plow to clear snow off the tracks. This stretch of the track was always a special problem because of the heavy, deep, blowing snows on Lizard Head Pass. In normal operations, two locomotives were usually enough to get just about any load up the hill. In this photograph, which was taken about 1910, there were seven locomotives needed to provide the required power to get through the extremely deep snow drifts. Several men stood on the tenders. They were undoubtedly used as snow shovelers. When the snow got too deep for even all this horsepower, they would hop off the train and help shovel through the cement-like snow. The train was probably just getting underway judging from the black smoke that was pouring out of all the engines. It took an unbelievable amount of hard work and money to keep the RGS Railroad operating all winter long.

RED MOUNTAIN SNOW

Two women and two children examined the large amount of snow that was still alongside the tracks of the Silverton Railroad in the middle of the summer in the late 1890s. Snow that remained in June or July was just as much an oddity then as it is now. The snow was probably the remains from a small slide that crossed the tracks of the Silverton Railroad just a few hundred yards north of Red Mountain Town.

Cⁿnimas Canyon Snow Plows

Denver and Rio Grande (D&RG) Railroad employees had hooked a snow plow to the front of several of their locomotives on this particular day so they could make a run at some of the more shallow areas of snow along the track in the Animas Canyon. As can be seen, the deeper drifts and avalanche areas had to be dug out by hand before the locomotive's plow could finish the work. At the point where a major avalanche crossed the tracks, the snow could pile up to sixty-feet deep, sometimes making snow tunnels necessary instead of cuts. Crews of over a hundred men might be called out to work on the job. Nevertheless, the Durango to Silverton route was often closed for months at a time in the winter because of the deep snows and avalanches. On a few occasions the people of the town of Silverton actually faced starvation or fuel shortages because of the blockages, since there was no other easy route between Durango and Silverton. Sometimes pack trains would fight their way out through the snow to Ouray in order to bring in supplies for residents or hay for Silverton's animals. (Ruth Gregory's uncles did such dangerous "mercy missions" on several occasions to help save the people of Silverton from hardships.) It looked like several women and children were watching this particular job of clearing the tracks, so it was likely that this was one of the first D&RG trains of the spring — fighting to break through and re-establish a link with Silverton.

${\mathscr{S}}$ILVERTON SNOW

Because of its high altitude, the snow can build up in
Silverton, Colorado, but not as much as shown in this distorted
view. Ruth copied the scene from a postcard labeled "Another
view of the last heavy frost in Silverton — 1931!" It was taken in
front of the French Bakery, which is still operating today. It can't
be said that Silverton residents don't know how to laugh at
themselves, especially in the winter when cabin fever sets in.

Steam Snow Shovel

After the invention of the steam shovel, the Denver and Rio Grande Railroad could bring one in mounted to a railroad car and pushed ahead of the locomotive. It then took much less manpower to clear a snowslide like this one photographed in the 1920s or 1930s on the route from Durango to Silverton. There still was a lot of manual snow shoveling required so the men on the left had shovels in their hands. The steam shovel wasn't running in this scene, a fact verified by the lack of steam coming out of the smokestack. The smokestack could barely be seen above the snow to the right. The man directly behind the steam shovel was talking to someone in the cab who was probably getting ready to start the shovel back up. From the absence of shadows it appears that the sun was high in the sky so it was most likely that the men had just returned from their lunch break.

𝒫LOWING FOR JEEPS

There is no longer any massive spring effort to plow snow for the local railroads, but there is such an effort to clear the jeep roads for the summer season. The San Juans have become one of the best mountain jeeping spots in the United States. Almost any day in the summer one can find a string of four-wheel drive vehicles winding their way up the old wagon roads to the top of one of the high mountain passes. It is some of the most beautiful and historic country in the world. However, the heavy winter snows would make many of the roads impassable until late summer if the counties and private individuals didn't plow them in the spring. This operator is nearing the top of Engineer Pass in early June during the 1960s. It is a rough and dangerous job since the driver can't actually see the road. An added hazard are the local marmots (a furry animal that many flat-landers mistake for a groundhog). Marmots love to eat the rubber items off of the dozers at night, which leaves cuts in the dozer's water and oil lines.

AUNTING FOR HUDSON BODIES

The Riverside Slide, which is located about four miles south of Ouray, is dangerous for many reasons. Primarily, it is actually two slides, one coming in from the west and one coming in from the east. Secondly, neither of the slides can be seen nor heard until they have dropped upon the unwary traveler like some giant cement truck that has just unleashed its load. Finally, the East Riverside Slide drops 3,200 vertical feet making the slide one of the longest and steepest in the United States. Over the years it has claimed at least eight lives and endangered many more. Although every death was a needless and totally tragic loss, perhaps the most heart-breaking of events was the death of the Hudsons on Sunday, March 3, 1963. Reverend Hudson lived in Ouray but he also conducted services for the Congregational Community Church in Silverton. On this particular Sunday, he had been told not to come to Silverton because of an extremely high avalanche danger. However, he not only decided to go but also made the choice to take his two young daughters, Amelia and Pauline, with him. When the tires started slipping near the Riverside Slide, he stopped his car to put on chains. It was a deadly mistake. A passing snow plow driver began to turn around to help him. All of a sudden the canyon was filled with flying snow. The slide hit Reverend Hudson's car totally without warning. The automobile and the three Hudson's simply disappeared into the snow. The snow was at a depth of forty to sixty feet in the canyon. Volunteers immediately began digging and probing for the bodies but to no avail. The next day metal detectors and St. Bernard dogs were brought to the scene. By Tuesday, the three small caterpillar tractors shown in these photographs were slowly moving the snow looking for bodies. It was a week before Reverend Hudson's body was found. Amelia's body was not found until March 17, and it was May 30th before Pauline's body was finally recovered. The car was found 600 feet downstream from the Riverside Slide with the doors and the top torn off. Surprisingly, however, a bottle of cream in the car was not broken.

$\mathcal{A}$UDSON CROSS

After Reverend Hudson and his two daughters lost their lives in the Riverside Slide, this cross was erected in their memory. The monument says it all: "This marker in memory of Rev. Marvin Hudson (and) his daughters Amelia and Pauline, who were swept to their deaths 1,000 feet north of this marker in the East Riverside Slide, Sunday, March 3, 1963. While answering the call to Christian duty of his pastorate in Silverton, Colorado. In honor of the many friends and neighbors who risked their lives to save them and recover their bodies. A symbol of the Christian faith that unites men in Christian love in times like these. Erected by the churches of Silverton, Ouray, Ridgway and the men, women and children who love these mountains." Next to it, unfortunately, is now is another monument honoring the three snow plow drivers who have been killed on the site since the Hudson's tragedy. The Riverside Slide remains deadly!

Chapter 6
From Burros to Railroads

TRANSPORTATION HAS ALWAYS BEEN THE CORNERSTONE of profitable mining in the San Juans. Plenty of gold, silver and other precious metals were (and still are) locked in the mountains. Often the problem was getting the ore to market and bringing in supplies in return — and doing so at a profit. In the very early days, the only way to travel in or out of the San Juans was by narrow, twisting trails. A burro could carry about 150 pounds along these routes, while a mule could transport up to 300 pounds. A large mine might require dozens of men and hundreds of animals for these tasks. Early transportation costs in the San Juans, therefore, ran from sixty to over one hundred dollars a ton, which caused only the very richest ore to be shipped.

Mules and burros were generally replaced by wagons as soon as proper roads could be built. Wherever wagon roads were constructed, shipping costs would usually fall to twenty-five or thirty-five dollars a ton. The costs were lower because a wagon could carry five or six tons of ore at a time and required only a single driver and six mules or large horses. In the winter, sleds were often used on the hard-packed snow. Wagon roads were quite often constructed as toll roads by private individuals since federal, state and local authorities had no money for road construction.

The railroad was the cheapest and most dependable way to ship ore and supplies. Most San Juan railroads used the little narrow gauge trains (three feet between the rails) since they could negotiate the steep curves that were necessitated by the mountains. When a railroad came to one of the San Juan towns, it marked the beginning of a new era. The railroad cut the cost of supplies in half as shipping rates fell to fifteen or twenty dollars a ton. Eventually the railroad itself was replaced by trucks and cars, which afforded greater mobility and convenience.

𝒞AMP BIRD PACK TRAIN

This panoramic shot from about 1910 caught a large mule train leaving the Camp Bird Mill in the middle of winter to take supplies to the mine at what was called Three Level in Imogene Basin. The pack train seemed to be transporting dynamite or powder and would probably take out ore concentrates on the return trip. The building behind the pack train was one of the Camp Bird's several boarding houses, but this particular one contained only sleeping rooms which were used by single men who were in management. Being typical bachelors of the time, there was no need for kitchen facilities. To the far left was a house that was used as a residence by the men in the Camp Bird's management who had families. It had a kitchen. To the right was what was called the "heating house," a part of the assay/smelting process. Further, down the road and behind the heating house was the Camp Bird recreation room and dance hall. The Camp Bird was a clean, well-organized "gold engine," according to Evelyn Walsh McLean, Tom Walsh's daughter. Others just called it a "class operation."

PACKING ORE CARS

Even as late as the 1930s it was often necessary to transport supplies and equipment to remote mines by mules or burros. These ore cars have not yet been mounted to their wheels, or they would have been too heavy for the mules. The cars also looked like they could possibly end up being attached to a tramway instead of mounted to wheels for use on track. The scene was probably in the Norwood or Placerville area. Even getting small items like this into the remote mountains took major effort if the items were heavy.

Labor Day Packing Contest

In the early 1900s, Labor Day was almost as big a holiday as the Fourth of July. Silverton celebrated with parades, contests, ball games and many other activities. In this photograph, Ruth Gregory's two uncles were participating in a mule packing contest held at the Silverton Labor Day celebration of 1912. The Shaw brothers won the packing contest easily. They pulled their suspenders down, stripped their shirts off and in their "long john" underwear began the contest. The object was to load onto mules the one hundred-pound sacks of lead concentrate ore that were stacked behind them. They had to load each of fifteen mules with four of the one hundred-pound sacks. Ruth's Uncle Allen is on the left and Uncle Ernest on the right. The man on the far left was Ledge Phillips. It was his job to lead each of the packed mules away when the Shaw brothers had finished tying on a load. Their winning time for doing all of the above was 4 minutes and 27 seconds!

ℬEAR CREEK TRAIL

Bear Creek Trail was one of the steepest and narrowest in the San Juans. As documented by the man and his horse near the middle of this photograph, the trail could be so steep and narrow that a rider would often prefer to dismount and walk. This particular trail was built by George Hurlburt in 1896 to upgrade the original trail on the other side of the canyon. The purpose of the improved trail was to give dependable year-round access to Hurlburt's Grizzly Bear Mine. The old trail (an Indian pathway first used by the whites in 1875) was on a north-facing slope. On that trail, snow quickly built up in the winter and made the trail impassable. It was totally uneconomical to try to do the necessary blasting to make either route into a wagon road, so mules and burros carried the rich Grizzly Bear ore to the mills in Ouray.

FREIGHT WAGONS ON CAMP BIRD ROAD

This long string of freight wagons, each pulled by six powerful mules, had stopped near the School House Slide to let the photographer take their picture. The time was most likely the late 1890s, and the wagons were probably owned by John Ashenfelter, the major freighter in the San Juans at the time. These wagons were heavy-duty; they had to be tough to be used on the rough mountain roads. The convoy seemed to be coming back empty after dropping off the Camp Bird or Revenue ore in Ouray. Because of the large output of the Camp Bird and Revenue Mills there was a tremendous amount of traffic coming into Ouray along the Camp Bird Road. Each of the above-mentioned mills shipped 300 to 500 tons of rich ore concentrates every day, seven days a week. In addition, another dozen or so mines transported ore along the road on a regular basis. The daily task required the use of fifty to one hundred wagons, as well as several mule teams and a whole herd of burros. Wagons, mules, burro trains and men on foot were strung out along the road all day long bringing supplies up the road to the approximately 1,000 men working at the mines and mills and bringing down the fruits of the men's labors. (This photograph showcases some of Ruth's artistic handwork. There was an almost non-existent image in the left lower quadrant, yet the scene was fascinating. Ruth took over fifty hours to draw in the missing parts, so that the photo was usable. She also hand tinted many of the photographs that she printed.)

Circle Route Stage

On this day, about 1900, the Circle Route Stage had stopped on the Million Dollar Highway with a full load of passengers, most of whom seemed to be awe-struck tourists. Even the ride on the stage was something unusual, since by 1900 the stagecoach had already become an oddity — a relic from the past that had been replaced by the train in most parts of the country. Tourists were usually quite pleased that there was a portion of the Circle Route that had to be traveled by stage, since it gave them a chance to relive the days of old. Another "oddity" that attracted the tourists was the local prospector and his burro. To quote from a 1913 brochure: "The famous old Concord stage is still used — drawn by six clattering horses, the driver picturesque on his seat....Likely enough a prospecting outfit, with pack train of burros, is encountered. At a certain point the stage from the other end is met and passed." In the scene at left a prospector can barely be made out behind his burro, leaning on the power pole. The highway was narrow; there was hardly room for the passengers to stand beside the stage. In many places it was absolutely impossible for two wagons to pass each other on the road.

Last Montrose-Ouray Stage

Someone, thankfully, remembered to get a photograph of the last stage from Montrose to Ouray on August 23, 1887. How often today do we take for granted what turns out to be the last of something? The stage continued to run for many more years from Ouray to Red Mountain. It was the railroad that made the Montrose to Ouray stagecoach obsolete. The Denver and Rio Grande Railroad didn't arrive in Ouray until December 15, 1887, but the stage company could already see the handwriting on the wall. Who would want to ride in the cramped, slow, dusty and cold stage when they could ride on the quick and comfortable railroad?

$\mathscr{B}$EAUMONT STAGE

The Circle Route Stage had just begun to get underway
after picking up passengers from in front of the Beaumont Hotel
in Ouray in the photograph above. The stage was being pulled
by six large and powerful horses. Every one of the six was needed
because of the steep climb to the top of Red Mountain Pass.
Besides being decorative, the bells on the two lead horses'
harness helped warn pedestrians of the approach of the stage.
The Beaumont was Ouray's premier hotel, built during 1886
and 1887 at the tremendous cost (for the time) of $85,000. It
contained forty-six sleeping rooms which rented for three to five
dollars a night. Its furnishings were lavish, and it contained a
beautiful two-story dining room and ballroom. The photo
depicts some changes which had been made since the hotel first
opened: the mansard roof which was added to either side of the
corner tower, some extra trim which was attached to the roof
peak and the trim on the building that was painted a different
color. The electric street light at the upper left of the photo dates
this scene to the turn of the century.

FREIGHTING TO THE VIRGINIUS

In the photo below, a large group of freighters was carrying timbers through Governor's Basin to the Virginius or the Terrible Mine, each located a considerable distance above timber-line at an elevation of 12,500 feet. The year was 1888. The logs could have been used for cribbing, firewood, mine timbers or a variety of other uses. Note that these weren't actually wagons; the logs sat directly on the wagon frame. The drivers, in turn, were sitting directly on the timbers without any type of seat. (It seemed like a good way to get some serious splinters in a very tender area. The driver on the last wagon was even standing up!) This was a rough and dangerous job. Current day jeepers sometimes get out and walk on these same roads. Hauling was only possible during the summer. In winter there were many times when this road couldn't be traveled by horses or mules, little less wagons. (This image was copied by Ruth from an old stereographic card, just one example of the various ways that she collected these historic images.)

ASHENFELTER TEAMS

Some idea of just how massive the John Ashenfelter freighting operation grew to be can be gained by carefully examining this photograph. Ashenfelter served both the Revenue and the Camp Bird Mills — each of which sent fifty or sixty tons of concentrates to Ouray and received in return an almost equal amount of supplies each day. He also carried freight and ore for many smaller mines. Ashenfelter, therefore, maintained barns and men at Sneffels and Camp Bird as well as his massive operation in Ouray. Just a few of his wagons are seen here, probably getting ready to leave one morning with the daily shipments. Only a portion of Ashenfelter's Ouray barns are shown on the left. There were many other structures connected with his operations in Ouray. Besides freighters, Ashenfelter had to employ veterinarians for his sick animals, ferriers for shoeing the horses, ranchers to provide hay and men to clean the stables. He also had a string of clerks just to keep track of freight and charges. In this scene, the Ouray railroad depot could be seen at the right rear and the building that currently houses the Silver Nugget restaurant was on the extreme left. The bridge that crossed the Uncompahgre River (to the left of the depot) was a constant source of embarrassment to Ouray's citizens. It was bad enough that it led into Ashenfelter's smelly barns, but it also passed directly through the middle of Ouray's Red Light District!

ℬURROS IN OURAY

This small group of burros was loaded with track which was used in connection with the lightweight mine cars at many of the San Juan mines. It was extremely light rail, ten or twelve pounds per yard of track. Only ore cars which carried a half-ton of ore (which was half the usual amount) could be used on the light rail. All of this downsizing was necessary because there were no roads to these mines, and the track and mine cars had to be brought in by mule or burros. The burros waited this day on Oak Street in Ouray before the house of George Wright. The house was originally built by Edward McIntyre in 1878 but was purchased the next year by the Wrights. It was first a log cabin but was covered with siding during the next year. Later, dormers were installed in the roof. George Wright and his brother, Ed, were very active in mining, so perhaps this burro train was on its way to one of their mines. The Wright brothers also built the Opera House in Ouray. As a booming mining camp, Ouray was then able to attract many plays, musicals and reviews as well as local productions. The Wrights were responsible in large part for bringing culture to Ouray. George Wright came to Ouray during its very beginnings, prospecting in the Imogene and Sneffels area in 1875 and then moving to Ouray in 1877. He located the Wheel of Fortune, U. S. Depository and Grizzly Bear Mines — all big producers.

CIRCLE ROUTE STAGE

This stagecoach (technically a Concord "mud wagon") was probably part of the Circle Route, a thousand-mile trip which began in Denver on the Denver and Rio Grande Railroad. Before the Rio Grande Southern (RGS) Railroad was finished in 1892, the Circle Route trip was made from Denver to Ouray by train and then by stagecoach from Ouray to Silverton where the trip continued on by rail. Even after the RGS was built, there were many travelers who preferred to take the alternate stagecoach trip because of the unforgettable beauty of the route and the total uniqueness of the ride in the stagecoach. The trip let them enjoy a form of transportation that had virtually disappeared in the United States after the advent of the train. This stage was overflowing with passengers. Since there are over twenty tourists, it is highly unlikely that they are all going to get on this particular stage. It was the era of the "roaring twenties" and everyone seemed happy and prosperous, except the stage driver, who seemed to be trying to keep his team under control.

ℳILLION DOLLAR HIGHWAY STAGE

The six horse Circle Route Stage had stopped at the "Ruby Cliffs," which is located about three miles south of Ouray (today half-way between Bear Creek Falls and the Engineer jeep trail cutoff) so that Leonore Wright could take this photograph. There were a few people on the inside, but note the expression on the face of the woman on top. Not only was she experiencing this hair-raising ride from high above the road on the tippy stage but she was also riding on the outside edge of the road at a point where the drop off is 300 to 400 feet straight down. No wonder she stared straight ahead! One tall tale of the naming of the Million Dollar Highway was that, after going over the road, one woman was reported to have said, "I won't go back over that highway for a million dollars." It could have well have been this woman who started the story. The stagecoach trip from Ouray to Silverton took about six hours. Today, by automobile, it is about an hour drive. Although much wider and straighter, the Million Dollar Highway still manages to thoroughly frighten many of the people who travel it.

Unloading Freight, Ouray

It looked like ore concentrate was being loaded into Denver and Rio Grande Railroad freight cars in Ouray for shipment to the smelters in Denver or Pueblo. The photograph below can be dated to the early 1900s because the Beaumont Hotel, the new City Hall and the brick school are all visible in the background. The arrival of the railroad made a huge difference to the output of the mines in the San Juans. Before the railroad, only the richest of ores could be shipped by wagon or mule train. Shipping costs could run as high as $60 or $80 per ton — even as high as $125 per ton from extremely remote areas, so ore had to be very valuable just to meet shipping costs. After the arrival of the railroad, the cost of shipping dropped to below $20 per ton, allowing ore that had previously been stockpiled outside the mines to be shipped. Unfortunately, the railroad arrived just a few years before the bottom dropped out of silver prices during the Silver Panic of 1893. Fortunately, however, gold was discovered in Ouray and Silverton at almost the same time, which allowed the towns to continue to thrive. The same trains that took out the ore brought in supplies and made travel easier all over the San Juans as well as to almost any point in the United States. After the arrival of the railroad, Ouray and Silverton were no longer isolated mountain towns.

ORE WAGONS, SNEFFELS

The photograph above of ore wagons getting ready to leave the town of Sneffels is one of the scenes for which Ruth gets the most requests for reproductions. These are D. C. Hartwell teams, and if one looks closely at the harness, his initials "DCH" are visible. Hartwell had a contract to carry ore from the Virginius Mine in the early 1880s. The wagon road had just been completed from Ouray and the ore was eventually shipped all the way to the Pueblo Smelting and Refining Company. The women in the photograph were identified as Mrs. Wright, Emma Wright and Mrs. Martin. The men were unidentified. The location of the scene was just above the little town of Sneffels. Normally women weren't involved with the freighting process; perhaps the women came along for the ride, since the road from Ouray to Sneffels included some of the most beautiful scenery in the world. That would make these wagons the forerunners of today's jeeps that tour Yankee Boy Basin.

JOHN DONALD FREIGHTER

In the photo below, mules had been loaded with large timbers for use in the mines. They stood before John Donald's barn and stables on Second Street and Fifth Avenue in Ouray. The ornate sign on his building read "John Donald. The Freighter and Packer. All Parts of the San Juan." The Beaumont Blacksmith Shop was next door to the left (south). The stables were originally built as the Beaumont Livery by D. C. Hartwell and William and Perry Weston — all prominent figures in early Ouray. The group also built the blacksmith shop next door, which still retained its original name at the time of this photograph. Directly across the street was Hartwell's brick office building. It was built in 1882 and was Ouray's first brick building. These establishments were used by the Circle Route Stage, but it was not an actual stage stop. They serviced the stage like a garage might take care of a bus today. The Circle Route picked up their passengers in front of the Beaumont Hotel.

CAMP BIRD STAGE

In the summer, the Camp Bird Stage was often an open carriage, as shown in the photograph below, instead of the closed conveyance that we often think of as a stagecoach. The passengers enjoyed the open air, the trip to Ouray was not long, and the scenery was beautiful along the way. While the men were in the back loading the luggage, the boy had taken the reins for the benefit of the photographer. A young girl, perhaps his sister, was already in the stage.

REIGHTERS

The driver of this team has been identified as Lyman Whitaker, the grandfather of life-long Ouray resident Gertrude Perroti. Mr. Whitaker brought the first safe to Ouray, where it was used by the first bank to be established in the new settlement. The Bank of Ouray was incorporated June 14, 1877, by Milton Cline, Jack Ohwiler, H. F. Blythe and H. W. Broloski. The bank occupied a building on Sixth Avenue, directly across from the present Ouray City Hall. It remained in existence until a few years after the Silver Crash of 1893. Mr. Whitaker was driving a "team of fours" in the photo above. The man standing in back of the wagon was operating the wagon's heavy brakes. The long, thick handle allowed him to put a great deal of pressure against the wheels. Still, it was often necessary when going down steep grades for the wheels to be chained so that they didn't turn at all. In some cases, trees (with all the limbs left on) were towed behind the wagon in an effort to slow it down.

ᴘACK TRAIN

This small train of burros was returning to Ouray loaded with ore from a mine in the nearby mountains. The burros were driven by a burro puncher and not led on ropes like the mule skinner did with his mules. It had obviously been quite some time since it had rained from the amount of dust that was rising from the road. From the position of their feet it also seems obvious that all of these animals were dragging, except the one to the far right, who was hurrying to catch up. It was about the turn of the century and the burro was being replaced by the horse-drawn wagon and the railroad. The little cabin in the background was a powder house. Ouray's miners used a small arsenal of dynamite and explosives in the mines each month. It was fairly common for fires to occur in Ouray since all heat came from wood and coal stoves. It was, therefore, against the law for any store to keep more than fifty pounds of powder in town. Even that amount could have taken out half a city block in a fire. The balance of the explosives were stored outside of town in cabins like this. Eventually the locals built a stone "powderhouse" at the beginning of the Camp Bird Road. It still stands at the southern entrance to Box Canyon Falls.

FREIGHTING A BOILER

Probably one of the most frequently asked questions heard by today's jeep tour drivers is, "How did they get that thing up here?" After driving slowly on an unbelievably rough road for an hour or two, the tour rounds a bend or comes over a hill, and there is some old, abandoned, gigantic piece of machinery. It seems utterly impossible that such a huge piece of machinery could be so high up in the mountains. How did they possibly do it a hundred years ago? The photograph to the right gives the answer. It took twelve huge draft horses to move this giant boiler. The driver didn't even have a seat; he just sat inside the boiler. Going uphill with this kind of load was dangerous, but going downhill was worse. The boiler had just gone down a small hill and chains that had been wrapped around the wheels were being taken off. The man in the back seemed to be checking the load to make sure that it was still securely attached to the wagon.

FIREWOOD HAUL

A herd of burros had been maneuvered to the Virginius Mine, high above timberline, with a load of firewood. The mine's boilers took these three- to four-foot lengths of firewood, much longer than logs for wood-burning stoves. It wasn't winter, but the Virginius had most of its supplies brought in during the summer while the trails were still passable. The burro puncher on the horse had driven the little animals, like sheep, up to the mine. Burros carried relatively light loads but could do it much cheaper than mules or horse-drawn wagons because they needed very little "storebought" food.

PIPE FOR THE VIRGINIUS

The photograph at left was taken by George R. Porter, who owned the store at Sneffels, Colorado and who was also an accomplished photographer. He took many shots of the activity in the vicinity of Sneffels in the late 1880s, but only a few of his photographs have been recovered. No one is sure what happened to his glass negatives. (Ruth copied this scene from a rare stereoptic view made by Porter.) Even in the summer it was usually necessary (because of snow) to transfer supplies to sleds for the last part of the trip to the Virginius Mine. The freighter on the left has been tentatively identified as George Newman. In this photo the cargo was pipe, which would be used to bring fresh air into the mine. In the background, on the left, was Stony Mountain; Teakettle Mountain was in the middle; and Potosi Mountain was to the right. The elevation was approximately 12,000 feet.

REVENUE PACK TRAIN

A pack train had just arrived at the Revenue Mill about 1910 to deliver a large load of timbers and perhaps drop off the sled full of firewood that was near the man at the front of the train. Lumber was always shipped a few inches longer than needed to make up for the amount that might wear off along the trail. The snow seemed to be about four-feet deep, which made it important for the burros to stay on the trail. In the background were the buildings of the little town of Sneffels and, in the distance, Stony Mountain.

$\mathcal{D}$ALLAS DIVIDE

A Rio Grande Southern (RGS) excursion train had stopped at the top of Dallas Divide, on the county line between Ouray and San Miguel counties, about 1950. Dallas Divide was officially named "Peak" by the RGS, but the name never caught on. Several of these trips were commissioned around that time by railroad buffs who knew that the RGS's life was drawing to an end. The passengers could travel in the coaches or ride in the gondola at the back where it was easier to take photographs. It looked like the stop at Dallas Divide was about to end as most of the people were climbing back on the train. Mt. Sneffels loomed in the background. The building on the right was a section house, while the structures in the back were barns and other buildings that were used for a nearby cattle ranch. There was also an employee bunk-house, stock pens, several sidings and a wye (for turning the train) at Dallas Divide. The rancher's home was behind the barns. Little stations like this were very important around the turn of the century when ranching and farming families used the train for access to the outside world. Only the stock pens remain at Dallas Divide. It is a shame the RGS's tracks were torn up. What a tourist attraction this route would make today!

RIO GRANDE SOUTHERN DEPOT, RIDGWAY

On this day (about 1950) the station master had parked his 1936 Pontiac "Chieftain" automobile under the eave of the Ridgway depot to keep it out of the sun. That it was his usual habit can be determined by the car showing up in virtually every photo taken of the depot at the time. The Ridgway depot was built by the Denver and Rio Grande (D&RG) Railroad, which then leased space to the RGS. The D&RG, as a trustee, also ran the RGS for most of its existence. As a result, much of the RGS equipment read "Denver and Rio Grande." RGS marked equipment is very scarce and valuable. The sign on the side of the depot, between the two windows, read "Rio Grande/ Royal Gorge/ Moffat Tunnel/ Scenic Line of the World/ Ridgway." The station agent and his family lived in quarters provided for them on the second floor of the depot. This was a very fine structure with many ornate details such as decorative iron balls on the roof, a corbeled brick chimney and large overhanging eaves with ornate brackets. This end of the depot contained the passenger waiting room. The old depot still exists in Ridgway, although it has been moved a short distance, turned ninety degrees and is now used as a residence.

OPHIR, COLORADO

This overview from about 1900 shows a remarkable scene that is very hard to capture on film — the little town of Ophir and the famous Ophir loop of the Rio Grande Southern Railroad. The town was built in the middle of a large loop which started up out of the Ilium Valley from the left and continued up the mountain to the right. The road to the power plant at Ames passed under the large trestle that was part of the loop to the left. The original town of Ophir was several miles up Howard's Fork Creek, but when the railroad arrived in 1891, many of the town's residents moved to this location, which was often called New Ophir, so as to distinguish it from Old Ophir. Old Ophir was established by Lieutenant L. Howard, after whom the creek is named. There are two versions about how the town received its name — one is that it was named after the biblical town of Ophir. The other version is that one of the first men to see the valley exclaimed "O fer God's sake, look at that!" The Ophir depot was near the center of this photo. Directly in front of the depot was a saloon and barber shop; to the far left was a general store; and between it and the depot were several strings of pack mules. To the right of the depot were homes and boarding houses. The road on the upper right led to the old town of Ophir. The site of the original Ophir depot (which was destroyed by an avalanche shortly after it was built) was in the foreground by the stack of logs.

ℜOTARY ON OPHIR

The Rio Grande Southern's (RGS) rotary plow was actively at work clearing wind-blown snow at the Ophir Loop on this wintry day. The photograph above was taken about 1900 from a spot close to the new town of Ophir. The RGS freight train, which had come down from Trout Lake, can be seen waiting for the tracks to be cleared in the background. The train then continued on its journey towards Telluride. If you look closely you can see a man standing on top of one of the boxcars. He was evidently trying to see how the snowplow was doing. The railroad engineers needed to be careful along this section of track because the snow and the ice caused many derailments. Some of the bridges on or near "The Loop" were a hundred-feet high, so it was much better to go slow and be safe. An old prospector's cabin could be seen above the bridge in the foreground. The bridge in the foreground went over the Howard Fork of the San Miguel River. Lt. L. Howard was the first white man to explore the Ophir area.

RED MOUNTAIN TRAIN

It was highly likely that T. M. McKee of Montrose was well-paid to come up and record the scene at Red Mountain Town on September 19, 1888. It was an exciting time for the citizens of the little community. The very first Silverton Railroad train had just pulled into Red Mountain Town and was unloading. Everything connected with the railroad was still pretty primitive. There wasn't even a depot yet, so this was where the passengers unloaded. The train only consisted of a locomotive, a Denver and Rio Grande freight car and a single combination car (half passenger seats and half baggage car) named "Red Mountain." The wye had not been completed, so all the train could do was back down the mountain. The passengers were being loaded into the Circle Route Stage (an open-air conveyance used at this time of year when the aspen were in their full fall glory) so that they can continue the trip down into Ouray. Other wagons were being loaded with the parties' baggage, which was quite considerable. Several celebrities were in this photograph. Otto Mears stood in front of the rear platform of the train and Ernest Ingersol, a famous eastern travel writer, was in front of him. The woman next to Otto Mears was his daughter. The identity of the lady in the checkered dress, near the center of the photograph, is unknown but she appeared to be carefully standing guard over her luggage.

BACHELOR SWITCH

The Bachelor Switch was an important Denver and Rio Grande Railroad siding located about a mile north of the present Ouray city limits. The Bachelor Switch was so-named because by throwing a switch, cars were left on the siding so that they could eventually be loaded with ore from the Bachelor Mine. Later the siding was used by other "Gold Hill" mines and mills — the American Nettie, Pony Express and Banner American. Bachelor Switch was also a spot where coal and supplies would be transferred into wagons for the final part of their journey to the mines. The road to the mines and mills can be seen going up the hill in the upper right of the photo. As can also be seen in this photo, a small settlement grew up around the Bachelor Switch siding. Quite a few people were waiting for the train on this particular day. There were some beside the track just in front of the train, others at the little section house (the small white building) and still others on the platform across the tracks. There were also passengers on the platform at the back of the train and people looking into the backwater to the left of the train. It was probably early summer as the Uncompahgre River was running extremely high.

OURAY DEPOT

These people might have been waiting for the train to arrive at Ouray's railroad depot which formerly stood at the spot of the present 4J's Trailer Park. Or perhaps they just agreed to pose for the photographer. The small coach to the right was used to take passengers to Ouray's better hotels, which were located several blocks away from the station. The depot was of typical Denver & Rio Grande (D&RG) design and was quite attractive. The north (left) end served as storage for freight. A scale and dolly stand by the freight door waiting to be put into service. The railroad agent's quarters were originally located on the second floor. The Ouray depot burned on May 20, 1948, four-and-a-half years before the "Ouray Branch" of the D&RG was abandoned. During the heavy spring runoff, the Uncompahgre River washed out a power pole which caused the electric lines to strike the telegraph line. This immediately sent 11,000 volts of electricity directly into both the Ouray and Ridgway depots. Fires quickly broke out in both places. The Ridgway fire was soon put out but $5,000 in damage had already been done. No one was in the Ouray depot, since the railroad agent had just recently bought a house and moved out of the station. The fire was not noticed until it was well underway. It was too late to do anything. The Ouray depot burned to the ground. Afterwards, a converted boxcar served as a depot until the line was abandoned in March of 1953.

OAK STREET CROSSING

The Denver and Rio Grande's (D&RG) engineer seemed to be taking but slight interest in the man and woman who were trying to cross the bridge over the Uncompahgre River ahead of the train. This particular bridge was located at the point where Ouray's Fourth Avenue would have been if extended to the Uncompahgre River. The short side track serviced the local Revenue Mine office and the mine's power plant, Rice Lumber Company, the Beaumont Sampling Works and several smaller establishments. The trail in the background led down from Oak Street to the railroad trestle, which was used as a shortcut to get to town, since the other bridges over the river were several blocks away. The north end of Oak Street was visible on the hill above the river. (The second house from the left and second from the right were lived in at various times by the Gregorys.) Directly behind the locomotive was the city's electric power plant. It generally used water to power its turbines but, when the water pressure was too low, the plant used coal for steam power. Hence the large smoke stack that was visible at the right of the photograph. The diamond stacked locomotive (here number 266) was typical of those used in the first years of the D&RG's operation in Ouray, dating this photo to about 1890. Since the Uncompahgre River was running high, the photo was probably taken in late May or June.

$\mathcal{M}$OUNTAIN SHEEP, OURAY

These mountain sheep had come down from the mountains to eat hay which had been left for them by the railroad employees. From this viewpoint it was obvious just how close they came to the railroad's operation. The Ouray depot could be seen over the top of the Denver and Rio Grande baggage car. The locomotive had been turned around on the man-powered turntable, hooked onto the cars and the men had climbed into the cab of the locomotive. It looked like the train was getting ready to leave. The sheep were purposely fed shortly before the train left so that the tourists could enjoy the sheep up close. Although the ewes were common, a big ram such as the one in this photo was not often seen at the railroad yard.

RED MOUNTAIN WYE

By the year 1890, when the photo below was taken, the railroad facilities at Red Mountain Town had been well developed. Red Mountain's depot was built right in the center of the railroad's wye, since there was no room for it in the actual town. A wye was a triangular arrangement of track that allowed the locomotives to turn around without using a turntable. It was the only known such placement of a depot in the United States. In addition to the unusual placement, the depot needed to be built on stilts as it straddled a small stream. The extreme northern end of Red Mountain Town's Main Street was on the far left of the photo. The small structure at the end of Main Street was the town's jail, built of two by fours laid sideways on top of each other. It was very sturdy and still stands. A freighter was unloading a boxcar and the Silverton Railroad's little locomotive No. 100 was turning on the track. In the background was the National Belle Mine which was built on a large hill called the "Knob." This angle made it obvious how the highly mineralized Knob got its name. The National Belle was one of the biggest and most profitable mines in the Red Mountain Mining District, mainly because it kept its expenses so low. Ore could be loaded directly onto the trains, and much of the National Belle's ore was found in soft deposits which could be shoveled straight into sacks without any type of blasting. The whole Knob was honeycombed with caves and caverns that contained all kinds of valuable minerals. They were beautiful and so unusual that many tourists came to Red Mountain Town simply to look at the mineral caves of the National Belle Mine.

FLOCK OF GEESE

The photo below, taken about 1910, shows the Rio Grande Southern's (RGS) business office (as opposed to the depot). As the great depression deepened, the RGS's revenues dropped drastically. Soon it was hardly worth the expense of sending out a train. In 1931 the RGS superintendent and chief mechanic came up with the idea of converting a Buick touring car into a rail bus. It was very inexpensive to run and to repair. It was officially referred to by the Rio Grande Southern as a motor car or a bus, but because it wobbled down the tracks, the name Galloping Goose quickly caught on. Not until almost twenty years later would the company officially adopt the name. The RGS's Galloping Goose quickly became a tourist attraction, although the funny-looking contraption had been conceived only out of necessity. Eventually there were seven of these geese hauling mail, supplies and tourists from Ridgway to Telluride and sometimes on to Dolores or Durango. The sign in the photo below was put up to attract tourists who might be traveling through Ridgway at the northern terminus of the railroad.

In the above photo, a whole flock of Galloping Geese had gathered in Ridgway about 1950. A part of the Ridgway depot could be seen to the right. It was summer, the tourist season, and there was a large group of rail fans on hand to be transported at least as far as the divide at Lizard Head and back. Each goose carried six to eight passengers in the "bus" up front. The rear section could hold another twenty or so passengers or 10,000 pounds of freight. If there were no derailments, animals on the track or rock slides, the goose made it from Ridgway to Durango in eight hours. The same trip can now be made by car in half the time, but it certainly wouldn't be as scenic. Some of the differences in construction of the geese could be seen in these buses, yet they all were basically hitched to the same type excursion car. The little gasoline car engines were relatively efficient to operate, much cheaper than a full-powered locomotive, yet the Galloping Goose had a real propensity for jumping off the rails. Usually the passengers had to get out and help leverage the contraptions back onto the track. In 1950 the last mail contract was canceled and regular passenger service was discontinued. The Galloping Goose prolonged the life of the Rio Grande Southern Railroad, but it wasn't enough to keep the line from eventually folding. Wouldn't it have been wonderful (and perhaps even profitable) if the Galloping Goose still ran today?

Casey Jones

The little rail motor bus pictured above served the same purpose that the Galloping Goose did on the Rio Grande Southern's Ridgway to Durango route, except that this car was owned by a mining company and ran on the Silverton Northern Railroad from Silverton to Animas Forks. It was named after the legendary railroad engineer, Casey Jones. For many years in the early twentieth century, the little rail bus carried passengers, mail and supplies to the Sunnyside Mine and Mill at Eureka, Colorado. It operated much more economically than a full-scale train. It was built in 1914 at the Sunnyside machine shops and was rebuilt several times over, the years. Its original purpose was to act as an ambulance, but since the bus seated eleven passengers, it was often used to transport men from the mine into Silverton for any number of functions. Its steering wheel was not used to steer but rather to activate its brakes. Originally a long chain ran from the flywheel to the rear axle to power the contraption. Later a drive shaft was installed. Casey Jones jumped the rails so often that jacks were built into its structure. When it jumped the rails, those aboard could then jack up the bus and shove it back on the tracks. The brooms were mounted at the front to sweep the rails clear of snow.

ᴌᴀsᴛ Tʀᴀɪɴ ꜰʀᴏᴍ Oᴜʀᴀʏ

It was a sad and snowy day when the last train left Ouray. The locomotive was actually arriving in this photograph taken March 21, 1953, but it was quickly turned around on the manual turntable and hooked onto a line of three boxcars which were full of Camp Bird concentrates, four empty coal cars and two boxcars that had been converted into the Ouray depot and station master's office when the original depot burned to the ground in 1948. Locomotive No. 318 of the Denver and Rio Grande (D&RG) then steamed away, hauling away with it virtually everything that was left of Ouray's railroad history. What had originally been the railroad's right of way was soon converted into a road from Ouray to Ridgway. In a few places the road doesn't exactly follow the old route, and a careful observer can still see a little bit of railbed. The D&RG's Ouray branch continued to operate from Montrose to Ridgway until 1977 when that part of the line was also abandoned.

MILLION DOLLAR HIGHWAY

This photograph showed the favorable condition of the Million Dollar Highway after the road had been upgraded from an automobile highway in the early 1920s to an even better road during the early 1930s. It still didn't look all that driveable but it was a great improvement! The rock retaining wall gave the travelers a much-needed sense of security. The road had not been widened to more than one lane, however. The stone barriers along the edge were added by the Civilian Conservation Corps (CCC) during the Great Depression. Today, many people who have just come over the highway ask why they didn't leave the barriers there. When this upgrade was done, the highway was not open in the winter. Therefore, snow removal had not been a consideration when the rock guard rails were added. During that time, snow was shoveled off the road by hand, if at all, and not by the big snow plows. Later, when the road was opened in the winter, the rock walls had to go because there was no easy way for the snow plows to push the snow off the highway.

The photograph was taken at the Ruby Walls, so named because of the color of the rock in the area. It has always been the steepest part of the Million Dollar Highway. This scene offers good views down the valley to the north of Twin Peaks. It was a postcard view — photographed, processed and sold by Al Moule of Busy Corner Pharmacy in Ouray.

JEEPING

Today, the four-wheel drive vehicle has taken over the same roads that were once used by the burro, mule and horse-drawn wagon. Jeep is a registered trade name but most locals still call it "jeeping." It is tourists who are now being transported instead of valuable minerals, but the positive effect on the local economy is the same. The Ouray Chamber of Commerce has for years raffled off a jeep to help cover its expenses. This particular prize was probably offered in the late 1950s or early 1960s. The little vehicle has opened up the beauty and history of the San Juans to many visitors who could never have experienced the awesome scenery by horseback or on foot. When combined with the incredible history of the area, the San Juans have rightly earned the title of "Jeep Capital of the World."

Chapter 17
Celebrations and Catastrophes

*W*HEN WE SPEAK LONGINGLY OF THE "GOOD OLD DAYS," it is often the recreational activities or the holidays that are brought to mind. Certainly it wasn't the back-breaking sixty- or eighty-hour work weeks or the large number of deaths and accidents. Rather, it was picnics, circuses, baseball games and the like that were fondly remembered. Holidays had special meaning in the remote regions of the San Juans. In those more patriotic times, the Fourth of July was a major holiday, sometimes lasting two or three days. Labor Day was also celebrated with great fanfare. Halloween was an exciting time of year. There were a lot more pranks or just outright vandalism than we have today. Christmas was a time of overwhelming anticipation for children. Quite often they received only "practical" gifts.

The local scenery and the wildlife did not go unnoticed by the local citizenry. Residents (especially the married or the engaged) took hikes, went on picnics or picked wildflowers. However, they usually did their exploring on horseback or burros instead of four-wheel drive vehicles. In the winter, snow shoeing, sledding and skiing were enjoyed by the young and old alike. In short, the residents of a hundred years ago enjoyed the San Juan Mountains much as we do today.

When we think of the olden times we also tend to remember the tragedies. The personal misfortunes, such as the death of a child, were always the hardest; but it was usually only the community tragedies, such as floods and fires, that got recorded on film. Government wasn't as big in the past as it is now, so there was a real feeling that it was up to each individual to help their neighbors in time of need. When the swimming pool flooded or the city hall burned, the townspeople simply rolled up their sleeves and went to work instead of depending on an insurance company or the federal government to take care of the situation.

OURAY BASEBALL TEAMS

Baseball was very popular in Ouray from the early days of the sport. Before the days of television, radio and videos, it was one of the main sources of summer entertainment throughout the San Juans. A baseball diamond was built at the present Ouray park well before the swimming pool or goldfish ponds existed. There were even covered bleachers on the site which could hold several hundred people. The fields were rocky and the pitchers were not great so the scores sometimes ran into the twenties or thirties. Ouray had both an amateur high school team and a semi-professional team. Large sums of money were wagered on both teams in their contests with the other San Juan towns. The top photo is of the 1908 high school team, complete with a bat boy, Fred Sibbach, who was in the center of the front row. Only about half the boys wore uniforms, a few wore padded pants and there seemed to be a general shortage of equipment. Just like today, there was a great discrepancy in the size of the players, depending on their maturity. The boys in the photo have been identified (back row, left to right) as John Clements, Roy Laird, Billy Wright, William Lee Knous, Sid Ashley and "Jink" Hughes. Left to right in the front row were "Toots" Van Houten, Otho Harris, Fred Sibbach, Sam Thistle and Roscoe Bradley. William Lee Knous later went on to become the Governor of Colorado, and his father served as the Ouray County sheriff for many years.

The lower photo showcases one of Ouray's many semi-professional baseball teams, this one from about the turn of the century. Only the man on the far left was an amateur. Each large town in the San Juans had its own semi-professional team. Citizens of one town would often travel a hundred miles to watch their team play. Sometimes large sums of money were paid to the players and even larger sums of money were bet on the games. Most importantly, this Ouray team won the summer series with Silverton! Nevertheless, there were only two of these players that had uniforms with the words "Ouray" on them. A couple of Ouray boys (complete with coats and ties) posed proudly as bat boys. This photo was taken at the southwest corner of the present ball field. The people in the background are on Main Street.

A GLASS OF BEER AT SNEFFELS

These men, who look like prospectors or miners, were having a glass of beer or wine in front of the hand-hewn post office and general store in the little settlement of Sneffels, Colorado. To a certain extent they were just showing off. This was an early day photograph, probably taken somewhere in the 1880s. It is believed that George Porter, the owner of the store, postmaster and an accomplished photographer was the man standing in the doorway. Most of the men held something in their left hands (as well as the drinks they hold in their right hands) as if they were celebrating an event. Perhaps it was the issuing of patents to their mines, location certificates for properties that they felt certain would make them rich, or perhaps just their pay checks? The little settlement of Sneffels was originally called Mt. Snefflels, after the nearby mountain that is the highest in the area. Mt. Sneffels is several miles away and can't actually be seen from the town of Sneffels. The 1890 census listed ninety inhabitants in the town of Sneffels but, with the opening of the Revenue Mine and Mill across the creek, the population swelled to 442 persons by 1900.

OURAY GUN CLUB

A few of Ouray's citizens had assembled at the Ouray Gun Club on March 14, 1909. These men took their sport seriously as they all carried professional target shooting guns. They also built a little club house at the range. The small pony cart on the left and the young boy on the right showed that children were also welcome. The Ouray Gun Club still exists today, but it is no longer at this location.

DUNBARTON PLUNGE

The Dunbarton Plunge (plunge is another name for swimming pool) was located at the same spot in Ouray as today's Weisbaden Hot Springs Lodge. It was built in June of 1884. Hot baths and vapor caves were always a favorite with the local miners, especially at a time when pneumonia, bronchitis and other respiratory diseases were prevalent. The establishment also rented hot baths — something miners didn't get to enjoy often, except at the big mines like the Camp Bird and the Revenue. In this photo the baths were at the left, the plunge at the lower middle (with new owner, Mr. Buchanon standing in front) and the Buchanon residence was at the rear. Mrs. Buchanon stood on the porch of their home and their little girl posed on the grass in front of the porch. Up on the hillside was a small cabin that stood on the spot of an even earlier adobe structure. In fact it looked like a part of the adobe home had been incorporated into the shed. The adobe structure was identified by an early-day photographer as the home of the famous Ute chief, Ouray (although Marvin Gregory argued vehemently that it couldn't be such because there is nothing else in Ouray's written history to indicate that Chief Ouray ever lived in the town which was named after him). To the left (on the hillside, above and to the left of the three trees) was a small cave and spring that were being used for soaking by the Indians when the whites arrived. There were also legends of Indian burials on this hillside. This hot spring probably had been enjoyed by the Utes for centuries before the white men arrived in Ouray's little bowl.

$\mathcal{M}$cLeod Bath House

Mr. and Mrs. John McLeod and one of their friends or guests (who sits to the left) appeared in this photograph taken in the sitting room of the building that housed their indoor swimming pool. The building was located on Sixth Avenue between Second and Main Streets in Ouray. The McLeod's world-wide collection of sea shells was prominently displayed in the cases that were placed around the walls. A good part of this sea shell collection is now in the Ouray Museum — an oddity at 8,000 feet in the mountains. The McLeod's had also decorated their lobby with framed photographs of local scenery. It could well be mid-winter, since the McLeod's used hot water which was piped down Sixth Avenue from the present-day Weisbaden to this location. The large pot-bellied stove undoubtedly did a fine job of heating the room. It sure looked like the dog was comfortable in front of it! A pile of towels for the McLeod's guests was stacked between the two of them. Decorations included a large book on the Revolutionary War to the left of the guest and flags from around the world on top of the display cases. An ever-present spittoon also sat on the floor by the stove. The McLeod bathhouse burned in 1950, but the various public and private hot caves and springs are still among Ouray's main attractions in the winter.

Early Tourists at Mineral Point

Even seventy or eighty years ago, Ouray, Telluride and Silverton enjoyed tourists, and they were just as interested in the history of the San Juans as the tourists are today. This group of early day "explorers" had stopped in front of the old Mineral Point post office. There is absolutely nothing that exists of this structure today, but wouldn't it have been fascinating to have explored it then? Mineral Point was one of the earliest and one of the highest settlements in the San Juans. It was first settled in 1873. The post office was not established until October 29, 1875. It continued in operation until abandoned on January 28, 1897. This photo was probably taken about 1910 or 1920. The town's name was derived from the extensive mineralization that can easily be seen running in veins across the surface around Mineral Point. Besides a post office, the settlement at one time had a store, a sawmill (even though the settlement was right at timberline), several saloons, and enough log cabins to shelter several hundred people in the summer. Mineral Point was known as "The Apex of the Continent," not because it was on the Continental Divide but rather because within a mile of its location were the headwaters of the Animas River, Uncompahgre River, Lake Fork of the Gunnison River and Henson Creek — all large streams that flow in different directions. One local justice, who was threatened with an appeal of his decision, reportedly remarked that he couldn't be appealed because there was no higher court than his. The settlement was at such an extreme altitude that it made a winter stay all but impossible. Mineral Point was totally deserted by 1900.

$\mathcal{B}$ox Canyon Trail

The early day trail to Box Canyon left the city of Ouray near the present Box Canyon Motel. It can be seen that the trail was a heavily wooded, beautiful walkway. It wasn't until 1936 that the present road was built from the south into the park as a WPA project. Perhaps Ouray's visitors lost something when this beautiful little trail was abandoned. The amphitheater rose above the trees in the background. Box Canyon was a local tourist attraction from an early date. The waters of Canyon Creek flowed over rock for almost two million years to sculpt a natural wonder. It was extremely difficult to get access into the canyon and to the actual falls until a wooden pathway for Ouray's hydroelectric plant was built into the falls about 1893. The structure held the pipe that fed water to the generators at the electric plant. Unfortunately it was soon discovered that mill tailings which polluted Canyon Creek ate away at the internal workings of the Pelton Wheel that produced the power. The intake was moved to the Uncompahgre River in 1902. The original structure which held the pipe then became a walkway into Box Canyon and gave excellent access to the interior where the falls is located.

FAMILY OUTING

The photographer caught two families out on a hike near the town of Sneffels on a beautiful summer day about 1900. The men probably worked at the nearby Revenue Mine or Mill. The view was taken from a stereoptican card. Two children, probably twins, ride in the saddle pouches of the burro. All of the women had brought their walking sticks along. The early day miners and their families loved the beautiful San Juan country much as we do today. They would send down reports that the wildflowers were in full bloom or that they had sighted big horn sheep. They loved to take long walks and go on picnics. Picking wildflowers was a favorite pastime (although please don't do so today, as we need them to go to seed so they can be enjoyed by future generations). Some of the miners even wrote poetry about their surroundings. Alfred Castner King, who was blinded in a premature explosion at the Bachelor Mine, became famous throughout the entire United States for his poetry and traveled widely reciting his poems from memory.

ELK AT THE ELKS CLUB

In the 1920s the Ouray Elks Club helped to sponsor an effort to reinstate elk into the mountains around Ouray. A game preserve was established in the amphitheater. Six elk were brought in and released into the local mountains. A feed rack was built on the nearby hillside and the Elks Club furnished hay. It seemed only appropriate that the elk should return the favor, and they often lounged on the lawn of Ouray's B.P.O.E. No. 492, as shown in the photograph below. Photographs like this were sent into *Ripley's Believe It or Not*, which evidently chose not to believe that these were real elk. The local herds grew quickly since there was no hunting season on the elk. They would often walk into town and graze at the City Park or along Main Street. In the winter of 1938, four large elk became so tame that they came to be considered pets by many of the town's citizens. The four elk hung around the town constantly for the next three or four years, and they were sometimes joined by others in the winter. Each of the four elk was given a name, with the largest being named "Solomon." When a hunting season was opened on elk, they naturally became much more wary. Elk can still be seen grazing near Ouray in the winter but they seldom come into town.

 IGH-WHEEL BIKES

These children posed by four high-wheel bicycles that had been parked alongside a house. They didn't ride these bikes (that was a man's job) but the children gave some idea of the size of the front wheel on these bicycles. They weren't easy to ride!

JIM THE BEAR

Shortly after the turn of the century, Jim the Bear was famous throughout the San Juans. In this photograph, taken near the end of his life, he was being fed by a woman friend. Dr. W. W. Rowan found Jim when he was a small cub and brought him home to be raised as a pet. Jim was a real attraction until he got to be this size. As would be the case with any wild animal, he simply shouldn't have been thought of as a pet. As Jim got bigger and rougher, Dr. Rowan evidently began to fear that he would do someone harm. So Jim was killed, stuffed and mounted so that he could be displayed in the back of Dr. Rowan's drug store on Main Street. Jim now resides at the Ouray County Historical Museum.

ℋALLOWEEN

These children had given up time from their Halloween party to allow a photographer to take their picture. Based on the nurse's costume, the photo was probably taken sometime around 1910 or 1920. There was an interesting selection shown here — most of these costumes wouldn't be seen today — and it was a virtual certainty that all of the costumes (except perhaps for the mask portion) were made by the children's mothers. A cowboy outfit was already a bona fide costume, even though these children lived in what could still be called the wild west. The black costume in the middle would certainly be inappropriate today. The nurse held a teddy bear for a patient. The boy who was second from the left in the second row was evidently a wizard or magician, and the girl at the top left of the photo dressed as a princess. Many of the other children are in what was kind of a generic costume that looked somewhat like a clown outfit, but which at the time was merely meant to indicate a costume. Several of the children wore no costume at all except for the face mask. The black mask was also a typical generic indication that you were in costume. The bunny wore a white mask. Several of the boys had tied a bandanna or cloth below their eye mask to further hide their identity.

$\mathcal{T}$INKER TOY MILL

This mill was evidently built by one of the miners or mill workers at the Camp Bird Mine. It was captured on film by Grant Marcy during the time he worked there (1900 to 1910). It was made almost entirely out of tinker toys and actually worked. It wasn't an exact copy of a mill, as it included a sort of windmill or Ferris wheel at the top and other little gadgets that came out from either end. However, it had all kinds of actual details like doors and dormers. It was driven by the little electric motor and wheel complex that was at the right of the photo. Evidently all kinds of things moved around when this contraption was in motion. Presumably the man standing next to it was the creator. The Camp Bird Mine tried to provide as much recreation as possible for its men. It was easy to get bored at the mines or the mills up in the mountains of the San Juans during the long and harsh winters. The project provided a diversion.

QUEEN ESTHER

A well known traveling company arrived at Wright's Opera House to present their production of "Queen Esther" on October 1 and 2, 1891. It was obviously a huge cast — especially for a stop at a small town like Ouray. Wright's Opera House quickly became Ouray's cultural center after it was opened in late 1888. The opera house was a large building that could hold several hundred people in its upstairs auditorium. The stage's original curtain hung behind the actors in this photograph. A copy of William Henry Jackson's photograph of the town of Dallas with the Sneffels Range was painted on the curtain. "Queen Esther" received good reviews in Ouray's *Solid Muldoon,* which reported that over a hundred voices participated in the rendition, which was under the direction of a Professor Bixler. The production drew a full house for both performances, which editor Dave Day reported to be "sufficiently meritorious to win universal approval."

$\mathcal{P}$RIZE FIGHT

This scene was obviously rigged; however, prize fights were extremely popular throughout the San Juan region about the turn of the century when this photograph was taken. Each town or large mine usually had its own champion and challenges were often issued in the papers to anyone who thought they could beat the local hero. Crowds of up to a thousand people would gather for some of the bigger fights, and prizes of a thousand dollars or more (half a year's wages) were not uncommon. The man in the middle of this scene was evidently the referee, and although the time keeper had been cut out of the scene, his watch appeared at the left of the photo. Everyone in the background seemed to be trying to keep a straight face. Both men wore "boxing belts." The little guy on the right had a real problem if hitting below the belt was not allowed during this match.

ELK AT THE SWEET SKIN

Ouray's tame elk liked to hang around the town in the middle of the winter because of the many hot springs in the area. Unlike the tourists, they didn't swim in or drink the water. Rather, they looked for the green grass that grew alongside the banks of the hot springs. It was easy to get to this food at a time when the snow piled up two- or three-feet thick over other edibles. These elk sported "mustaches" from foraging for food in the snow. The Sweet Skin resort was located close to today's Box Canyon Motel. It advertised that its "radioactivity" was thought to be helpful for a variety of ills. Tourists would soak in and drink the water for its curative properties. Actually the radioactive content was quite low — far too little to help or hurt anyone. Today the FDA would never allow a claim that the water "cures diseases and restores health." The sign even gave a helpful hint on how to pronounce the town's name (You - Ray) — a problem that is still shared by many of Ouray's first time visitors.

OURAY POOL

These early day Ouray pool scenes were shot in the first part of the 1930s. The pool had been built in 1925, but unfortunately the hot water in the area was not sufficient to fill it. It was two more years before hot water was piped in from a hot spring near Box Canyon. The bath house, shown here in the photo above, was completed a few years later. The pool originally advertised itself as "The Radium Springs Park — Natural Hot Water Pool." At the time, radioactivity was thought to be healing; so Ouray also advertised the pool as "the most radioactive on the American continent," even though it actually contained only very low-grade levels of radioactivity. People were encouraged to drink the water to cure a variety of ills, including rheumatism and arthritis. Picnic tables, benches, tall trees and grass surrounded the pool. The pool and park were a great place to come in the summer to spend the day. It wasn't open in the winter. Ouray's citizens even installed a water slide, seen here to the left of the bath house doors in the photo above. Outside electric lights also surrounded the pool. It was a very popular spot that immediately drew people from as far away as Silverton, Montrose, Delta and Telluride. It still does, especially since the pool is now open in the winter.

OURAY HOSE CART COMPANY

About 1905, the Ouray Hose Cart Company proudly posed in front of the Ouray City Hall on the Fourth of July. Everything, including parts of City Hall itself, had been wrapped in crepe paper. A few of the men have been identified. At the left with the fire bugle was Tom Mowalt. He was a prominent Ouray citizen in the early days. Others in the photo who have been identified were Con O'Burns, Joe Finnin and Jack Boast. The hose carts were kept in the City Hall building. The "pumper engine" was run by steam. It was cranked up and ready to go in this photograph as a little smoke curls out of the chimney.

CASCADE FALLS

This fantastic winter scene of Cascade Falls was taken late in the season when the ice had plenty of time to form and thaw so that it broke loose and cascaded down the mountainside. The boy, woman and dog at the left center of the photograph gave an excellent sense of proportion to the scene. It is often hard to catch the immenseness of the San Juan Mountains and the towering cliffs. Tourists often take roll upon roll of pictures; and then after the photographs are developed, they find themselves commenting that the snapshots just can't do justice to the awe-inspiring scenery. Frank Rice usually did a wonderful job of capturing the correct proportions of a scene such as this one, and in this photo he did it in a very artistic way.

Horses on Horsethief

Horsethief Trail takes its name from the thieves (both white and Native American) who stole horses in the San Luis Valley and used this path to take them to Utah. The local section of the route offers some of the most beautiful but remote scenery in the San Juans. Many hikers have called it the most scenic trail in America. It is quite a scary horseback ride, especially as shown above at the Bridge of Heaven, which is only a few feet wide. On either side there is a drop of almost 3,000 vertical feet, yet a person can see all the way into Utah. Inexperienced riders usually get off and lead their steeds across this part of the trail. It has always been a trip that was worth the effort.

Horseback at Camp Bird

It looked as if these riders had come up to the Camp Bird Mine for the day. The women all rode side saddle as proper ladies would do at the time. The Camp Bird's large mill could be seen in the background. The buildings behind the riders were residences for the families of some of the management, so it is likely that the group may have come up to spend the day with friends. The dark building to the right of the mill was one of the Camp Bird's famous boarding houses, which contained all the amenities that its mill workers could have hoped for.

BEAUMONT HOTEL

The photograph below of the Beaumont Hotel was shot shortly after it opened in 1887. The citizens of Ouray were rightly proud of the hotel, as it was certainly one of the finest in all of Colorado. Several of the hotel's guests or visitors watched the photographer out the southern windows, which were open to catch the breeze on this fine summer day. The doorway to the right side of the hotel was the "ladies entrance." It was separate from the front entrance, which was also used for the entryway for the bar and billiards rooms. It was thought inappropriate for any lady to be in one of those establishments. The ladies entrance was used to get to the dining room, in which were held some fabulous dances and dinners. Most of Ouray's Main Street was visible to the left. Especially noticeable was the two-part flagpole, which had a speaker's stand constructed about six or eight feet up from the ground. It was a favorite spot for long, patriotic Fourth of July orations. The flagpole was taken down in 1903. The Beaumont had long been the center of Ouray society. What a shame that it remains closed today!

MILLION DOLLAR HIGHWAY

Frank Rice loved to take his automobile up on the Million Dollar Highway both in the winter and in the summer. He was also a loving, family man whose passion was photography. So it is not surprising that many of his photographs were taken of his car and his family on the Million Dollar Highway. In the top photo it was the heart of summer and the hood has been taken off Frank's car. It was a favorite trick of the time to help keep the early day automobiles from overheating on the steep highways. There was also a bucket hanging off the left side of the car, allowing Frank to stop at any one of the little mountain streams along the road to replenish the water in his radiator. He had kerosene lights on the sides of his car as well as the electric lights in the front. This duplication was a leftover from the carriage lights that went on buggies and wagons. Frank also had the crank mounted on the front of the car. No dead battery on this car!

Judging by the license plate, the bottom photograph was taken in 1927. Frank's wife, son and daughter had accompanied him on this snowy day as far as they could get on the Million Dollar Highway before the car was stopped by the snow. The skinny tires actually worked well in the snow so, even though the car was not a four-wheel drive, the Rice family had made it a fair distance.

ℬ OOTLEG WHISKEY DESTROYED

Even though the San Juans voted overwhelmingly to the contrary, Colorado went dry on January 1, 1916, some three years before the Eighteenth Amendment to the United States Constitution made liquor illegal throughout the entire United States. The locals didn't accept the change easily, and many of the people in the San Juans began bootlegging operations. It was almost impossible for the federal authorities to find liquor distilling operations in the rugged mountains and the bootleggers prospered. These two photographs chronicle the final chapters of one bootlegger's story. The liquor had been seized by Sheriff Krisner at the home of a Mr. Faletti in March of 1916. A raid had been made on the premises after many locals reported that he was carrying on bootlegging activities on a large scale. County Judge MacAdams sentenced Faletti to three months in jail and ordered the illegal liquor destroyed. The May 15, 1916 *Ouray Herald* reported that "two years ago a conviction of this character would have been practically impossible to obtain in Ouray county, but at this point sentiment has changed to a point where ninety per cent of our residents heartily approved of the verdict of the jury finding Faletti guilty and also of the destruction of the liquor." The paper also noted that a number of pictures of the scene had been taken and were selling rapidly.

These are two of those photographs. Between seventy-five and one hundred people were reported to have congregated at the Ouray Courthouse as the sheriff removed the confiscated booze. The amount and diversity of liquor was incredible: one full barrel of whiskey, one case of bottled beer, ten bottles of beer, a half-empty barrel of whiskey, ten gallons of sherry, ten gallons of gin, forty-eight bottles of whiskey, eight quart bottles of claret, eight quarts of wine, six bottles of burgundy, thirty-one bottles of mixed liquor, two quarts of XXX Kennessy, two bottles of Gordon malt, and four bottles of Benedictine. The liquor was valued at over $450 (more than $10,000 at today's value). As employees and residents watched, the sheriff took the liquor from where it had been stored in the basement of the courthouse. Then it was loaded onto a wagon which was taken to the corner of Main Street and Sixth Avenue. At that point the offending booze was poured into one of the few storm drains that existed in town and eventually ended up in the Uncompahgre River. As can be seen from the photographs, the majority of the crowd was composed of children. Apparently, no women felt it respectable to be present. Perhaps most of the men were at work or maybe they couldn't bear to watch!

Fourth of July Float

Schwend, Mostyn and Lupher, local Ouray grocers, sponsored this cute little float for the Fourth of July parade about the turn of the century. Goat carts were extremely popular at the time — in fact almost any type of miniature was popular. Two very fancy goats pulled this cart. The boy at the right was dressed in the type of costume that children would wear to a costume ball or to dress up for a party, while the two children at the left were elegantly dressed as their parents might be at the time — right down to the parasol and the top hat. The boy held reins to the goats (which were probably useless) and a buggy whip (which was probably well used). The little wagon had been decorated to the gills — crepe paper everywhere and a large American flag at the top. The float may well have won a prize. At least it struck the photographer's fancy.

FOURTH OF JULY WATER FIGHTS

Water fights on the Fourth of July are a long-standing Ouray tradition which is still carried on. This particular contest was probably held in the 1920s. The spectators have always loved to crowd in close to the fight and get sprayed by the water. The fights have usually been held at the corner of Sixth Avenue and Main Street, which was the case in this photo. Today the participants use helmets, face masks and heavy suits, while these contestants used only rain hats and rain coats. However, they were also using a smaller hose and the water pressure wasn't as great as it is today. The winners of the water fights have always received a monetary prize. The prize was comparatively larger in the past than today. However, these "old-timers" faced a hazard that we don't have at present. The city took its water out of the city reservoirs, which were open ponds, and as a result the water often carried small rocks and pebbles. Quite a few of the old time water fights were, therefore, stopped when one of the participants started to bleed badly enough that it looked like the fight shouldn't continue. Today's participants face the dangers of high water pressure; contestant's helmets have been blown off their heads by the water, and several people have nearly drowned before the water was turned off. Whether in the past or the present, the contestants in these fights certainly earn their money!

JULY 3, 1897

The Deutsch Brother's grocery and delivery wagon had been decorated for the Fourth of July parade of 1897. The owners had stopped outside their grocery store on the 3rd of July to have the above photograph taken. For this particular Fourth of July, the planning committee came up with the idea of decorating the town like a winter wonderland. They cut little evergreen trees to line both sides of Ouray's Main Street. A small American flag was placed at the top of each tree. They also planned to have wagons bring down snow from high in the mountains to place along Main Street. But on July 3rd, it snowed an inch or two in town! Ouray's weather never ceases to amaze its residents. Perhaps this event disproves the saying that Ouray has only two seasons — winter and the Fourth of July. The grocery wagon carried a lot of goodies including strawberries, which were probably from Paquin's huge strawberry farm on Corbett Creek to the north of Ouray. The wagon and horses had been heavily decorated with flags on the horses' heads and on the boy's hat.

The men in the photo below had retrieved their snow shovels from wherever they had stashed them for the summer. This July Third morning was cold, really cold. So the men put on their coats and raised their collars and went out to shovel the plank sidewalks. There was only an inch or two of snow, so they decided, as many grown kids do, to try to get enough snow in one spot to make a snowman, or at least to have some good fun throwing snowballs. The photographer (probably Brumfield, who had his studio just around the corner on Sixth Avenue) saw this scene early in the morning on Main Street and just had to get a photograph. Snow in Ouray on the Third of July. Who would believe it! Well, anyone who saw this photo in the years to come would believe it. Unlike some people, photographs don't lie.

Ouray City Hall Reconstruction

It was one of Ouray's saddest moments when the city hall and library, patterned after Philadelphia's Independence Hall, burned to the ground in 1950. It was a total loss and most of the town's people literally wept. Times were tough then, and the citizens of Ouray had to make do with what they had. Unfortunately, that did not include insurance proceeds on the building so city hall was rebuilt with volunteer labor. (Marvin Gregory worked extensively on this project.) Not only was the building a total loss but so were its contents, including many rare books and pieces of art that had been donated to the citizens of Ouray by Tom Walsh, owner of the famous Camp Bird Mine. Walsh had also given the second floor of the building, which was used for a library. The bell that Walsh gave the city cracked in the fire but was saved and now sits in a place of honor before City Hall. In this photo, the workmen had built a small wooden hoist to get the new steel roof joists into place. Even with a total lack of funds, Ouray's citizens had rebuilt the city hall and library within a year of its destruction. However, they were not able to copy its original form. In 1988, Ouray was able to again redo the city hall in such a way as to almost exactly duplicate its original architecture.

ℱLOOD OF 1909, OURAY

Cascade and Portland creeks have always had flooding problems. In 1909, a major flood hit Ouray and brought considerable debris down and around Main Street. This type of flood seems to occur about every twenty years or so, the last being in 1982. The problem associated with these floods has usually been the debris that is brought down from the mountains and not the water. Major work has now been done to widen and deepen the flumes that carry the creeks, but only time will tell whether it really works. This photo was taken shortly after the Elks Club, at the left in the scene, was built. The building to the right of the Elks Club was a ladies clothing store. The sign on the side of the building looked like it could read "Clossin Saloon," but it could also be a "Closing Sale" sign. It certainly would have been reasonable to have a closing sale after this kind of mess. As bad as this scene looks, Ouray has always quickly rebounded from its floods, usually returning to business as normal within a few days.

$\mathscr{M}$UCKING OUT THE POOL

Ouray's hot springs pool certainly had its share of troubles in its early years. The land for the pool was purchased in 1914, and picnic tables and fish ponds were soon constructed. A couple of alligators were even released into the fish ponds and they thrived. Nothing was done about building the swimming pool proper until 1923. At that time a drive was mounted that raised the money for the pool. Ouray's citizens worked for two years to finish the project. However, when the pool was finally completed, it was discovered that there was not enough hot water available from the immediate area to fill the swimming pool. It took another two years of fund raisers and contributions before hot water could be piped in from the vicinity of Box Canyon, which was over a mile away. Ten little cabanas with wooden sides and canvas tops were built around the pool to be used for changing rooms, and the pool finally opened in 1927. Only two years later a flash flood caused both the Uncompahgre River and Skyrocket Creek to overflow, which filled the swimming pool with several inches of debris. The flood also washed the cabanas, the fish and the alligators down the river. Money was very tight because of the 1929 stock market crash, but Ouray's citizens again rallied and not only cleaned out the pool, as seen in this photo, but also finished the permanent bath house (shown to the left in this scene) by the next year. The pool was an immediate a hit and has always made a good profit.

CHRISTMAS DAY

It was Christmas in Ouray sometime circa 1915. As with all Christmases, it was a time of excitement and wonder for these children, who appear to have gotten up early this morning to discover that Santa brought a new tea set, a drum, a doll buggy, a doll and a toy car. What a wonderful tree, certainly cut from close by in the mountains surrounding Ouray. The unusual ornaments included gloves, an infants' shoes, socks, pot holders and lace handkerchiefs among other items. Perhaps that was just an unusual way to display some of the presents. These children, whom Ruth believes to be Betty and Edward Creel, obviously lived in an ornate "Victorian-style" house. Betty became a school teacher and was Noel Gregory's first grade teacher.

CIRCUS IN OURAY

The circus was in town on this exciting summer day about the turn of the century. Almost every summer during the early 1900s a small carnival or circus visited Ouray. Children lined Main Street's sidewalk, but the parade actually started on Fourth Street between Fifth and Sixth Avenues. Many of the children's parents and other adults looked on. This was a time of major excitement for the community. The procession hadn't reached the big crowds yet, which would have gathered to the left (north) on Main Street. A small elephant led the parade, followed by several circus wagons that certainly included lions or tigers. Several Ouray churches are visible in this scene. The Methodist church was the white frame building on the northwest corner of Fourth Street and Fifth Avenue. The Episcopal church's bell tower could be seen on the opposite side of Fifth Avenue. The Rose brothers' survey office stood in front of the Methodist church and the J. J. Mayers Mercantile Company blocked the view of the Episcopal church.

Early Day Car Wreck

Even though the old Model T's didn't go as fast as today's cars, they still had their share of wrecks. This automobile ended up in the Uncompahgre River at the lower bridge into Box Canyon. Ropes had been let down into the river to begin the process of bringing the automobile back up or perhaps to make sure that the car didn't get washed farther down the river.

$\mathscr{P}$RESBYTERIAN CHURCH

In the scene above, half of Reverend George Darley's little Presbyterian Church was rounding the bend by the swimming pool in Ouray on its way to Nucla, Colorado. The little frame building began its life in Ouray in 1877. It was Ouray's first church building, and the Reverend Darley did much of the work himself during the initial construction. It was built on the site of the present Catholic church; and when it was dedicated on October 14, 1877, it became the second church structure on the Western Slope of Colorado (the first was in Lake City). However Reverend Darley did not become the local minister and perhaps because of that (he was extremely popular), the Presbyterian church faltered. Things got so bad that their building was eventually sold at a foreclosure sale in 1883. The building and land eventually went to the Catholics, who used it for many years. In the 1950s, as the Catholics grew in numbers, the building was sold to a church in Nucla and the Catholics built their present stone structure. The Presbyterians rallied in Ouray and at present are by far the largest of Ouray's five churches. It all goes to prove one of the favorite sayings of San Juan residents: "What goes around, comes around."

CONCLUSION

As you have seen, this book is a collection of San Juan scenes from the past. The San Juans are still making history, especially in the last decade as they are again being discovered by the outside world. The rich and the famous flock to Telluride and Purgatory. Durango, Silverton, Ouray, Rico, Dolores and Ridgway are all growing rapidly. Much of the rich minerals that drew the original prospectors to the San Juans still lie within the bowels of the rugged mountains waiting for discovery. Some day the prices of gold, silver and other rare metals will rise and there will again be significant mining activity in the area. Tourism, development and mining may compete in times to come. Hopefully, we will use our knowledge of the past and experience in the present to successfully handle any conflicts.

Hopefully, too, there will be more people like Marvin and Ruth Gregory who will take the time and effort to accumulate a collection of photographs or videos or oral histories that will preserve the essence of today's culture for those of the future. It is still important for us to remember that the present and the past are only separated for an instant in time. Today's events are tomorrow's "good old days." We learn from the past and we should record the present in order that the lessons of today will be available for the future.

INDEX